I Don't Remember My Father's Face

A Memoir

Melenaite Uata Sr and 'Uliti Uata

I Don't Remember My Father's Face: A Memoir

Copyright © 2022 by Melenaite Uata SR and 'Uliti Uata

All rights reserved. No part of this book may be reproduced or transmitted in any form or by any means without written permission from the author.

Library of Congress Control Number: 2021925822

ISBN 979-8-9855090-3-8 (hardback)

ISBN 979-8-9855090-0-7 (paperback)

ISBN 979-8-9855090-4-5 (epub)

Unless otherwise indicated, Scripture quotations are taken from *The Holy Bible: King James Version.*

Cover design by Victor 'Unga

Cover background photo by Salome Uata

Printed in USA by Douglas Publishing/Portland, OR

Dedication

In loving memory of my father, Lisiate Mafi Uata, whom I've idolized even without remembering his face.
To my brother, Venisi Uata, who sacrificed so much on my behalf. The fabric that weaved the bond of our friendship was composed of love, respect, and trust.
To my beloved mother, Melepua Finau Uata, whose fierce determination and grace radiated light of hope through her eyes. Come what may, her strength and tenacity were the glue that held our family together regardless of our circumstance. I dedicate this book to you, for an unforgettable journey and for helping me discover my life's purpose. May you rest in peace until we meet again at Heaven's gate.

Map of Tonga

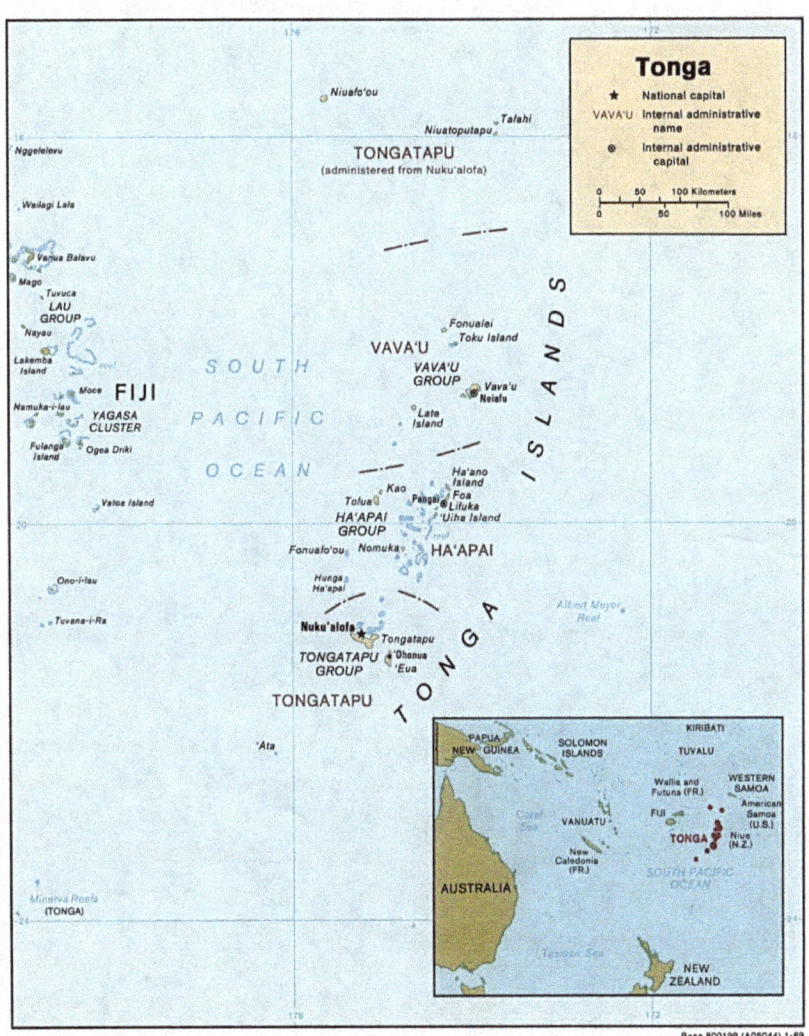

Image courtesy: https://upload.wikimedia.org/wikipedia/commons/d/dd/Tonga.jpg

Table of Contents

Dedication 3
Map of Tonga 5
Acknowledgment 9
Prologue 11
Introduction 13
Chapter 1: The Long Walk 15
Chapter 2: A Boy from Ha'ano 23
Chapter 3: Unchartered Territory 33
Chapter 4: Forward and Onward 41
Chapter 5: Humble Beginning 51
Chapter 6: Rescued 59
Chapter 7: $19 Legacy 69
Chapter 8: Unexpected Miracle 77
Chapter 9: Year of the Dragon 85
Chapter 10: Lighthouse of Hope 93
Chapter 11: Conquered Crossroads 101
Chapter 12: Pivotal Moment 109
Chapter 13: Ocean of Dreams 119
Chapter 14: S. O. S. 129
Chapter 15: Deep Roots 137
Chapter 16: Political Arena 145
Chapter 17: Far Reaching 159
Chapter 18: Floating Grave 169
Chapter 19: Breaking Point 181
Chapter 20: Discovered Treasure 193
Chapter 21: Acres of Diamonds 201
Chapter 22: Mausoleum 211
Chapter 23: Unsung Hero 223
Family Photo Album 237
Images of Tonga 241
References 243

Acknowledgment

Where do I begin to acknowledge the countless people who have filled my life with meaning? How do I express my gratitude? I will list a few but know that so many people not mentioned on this short list make up the totality of my life experiences.

- To my Heavenly Father whose invisible hand has been present throughout my life. From the peak of the mountain to the valley floor and everything in between; and to my Savior, for His love and atoning sacrifice that saved even a sinner like me.
- To my loving wife, Lu'isa Mataele Uata, who saved our family with her resilience, resourcefulness, endurance, forgiveness, and faith. Her life is a reflection of her beliefs and embodies Christ-like love.
- To my niece Seini Toakase Finau Folau for your help in raising our children and supporting me for years with the business. And to the rest of the Finau children, our adopted children.
- To Edward Kay Uata for your cooperation and years of faithful service, in dedicating your skills as an engineer to help run our family's ferry boat business.
- To the late Takilesi 'Ofa-ki-Ha'angana Uata and his wife, Salome Malu Uata, and his two children, Walter 'Ofa-ki-Ha'angana Uata and Monalisa 'oe Maka-ko-Fele'unga Uata for being by my side and helping to take care of me after my stroke and for continuing to this day.
- To Melenaite Uata Sr for helping me write my life's story and co-authoring this book.

- To Vosa Taka and 'Ofa Taka for helping me with parliament campaigns in Ha'apai.
- To the late Prime Minister of Tonga and my dear friend, Samuela 'Akilisi Pohiva, for sharing my passion and vision as we worked together for more than three decades in parliament serving the people of Tonga.
- To Dr. Tevita Tu'i Uata for following my footsteps into politics and being a public servant by using his God-given talents to serve in his capacity as a Minister of Labor and Finance.
- To all my friends and colleagues of the Tongan Parliament Assembly for sharing your wisdom and gifts to help build up our Island Kingdom.
- To all the supporters of the Liahona Alumni Association, who have contributed so much of your time, money, and resources to this worthy cause.
- To the people of Ha'ano, Ha'apai for trusting me to carry your dreams and allowing me to represent your voices to the government.
- To my precious family, my children, Venisi Uata Jr, Dr. Mele Lavinia Uata Fangupo, Melenaite Uata Sr, Dr. Tevita Tu'i Uata, Thomas Monson Uata, Edward Kay Uata, Mele Lupe Uata Tangi, Takilesi 'Ofa-ki-Ha'angana Uata, 'Afa Paea-i-Vahamama'o Uata, Melenaite Uata Jr Ta'ai and Lucynita Murley Uata Tafolo; and to all my grandchildren, great-grandchildren, and future generations of the Uata family. Thank you for filling my life with happiness. You truly are my timeless treasures.

I thank you all for your help, support, friendship, and love. We have shared both laughter and tears for many years, but through it all, you have made a difference in my life, which allowed me to endure even the worst of times and experience joy beyond compare in the best of times.

'Uliti Uata
Spring 2022

Prologue

Nuggets of wisdom learned throughout my journey…

- Life unexplored is being alive but not living…
- Life imagined is dreaming instead of doing…
- Life undiscovered is being gifted but not recognizing it…
- Life wishful thinking is following instead of leading…
- Life pleasure is service—giving love and receiving love…
- Life treasure is family—knowing that you belong…
- Life challenge is not rising up to your God-given potentials…
- Life puzzle is looking for happiness when the power lies within…
- Life regret is wallowing in self-pity instead of being proud of who you are…
- Life blessing is performing acts of kindness and making a difference to someone else…
- Life secret is searching for meaning and discovering your purpose…
- Life is both unpredictable and magical; embrace this moment to its fullest, for tomorrow is never promised…

Introduction

July 10th, 2012, I woke up unable to move. I was rushed to the Vaiola Hospital in Tonga and learned I had had a stroke. My world was turned upside down. This was a reality that reawakened my sense of mortality. I learned to adapt to my new life wheelchair-bound. My mind became clearer as the details of my memories sharpened. I felt compelled to share my story, not only for the future generations of my family but also for whomever will read it, so that they may be inspired to look at their own journeys through self-discovery.

Following my stroke, I could no longer use my hand to write down my thoughts, and my speech slowed with my medical condition; yet it also served as a call for action. I outreached to my children for help. Eight years had lapsed with no progress; yet my faith waxed strong with a firm conviction that if there's a will, there's a way. The urgency to put my story on paper heightened with

Introduction

each passing day. On August 5th, 2020, I awoke with a prompting to reach out again to my children.

One of my daughters, Melenaite Sr, answered the call as she felt my burning desire even when we were thousands of miles apart. She did a video chat from America, and she said as she choked up with emotions, "Dad, I'm sorry that I've ignored your request to write your story for so long simply because I do not have the educational background. Although I feel inadequate in every sense of the word, I can no longer ignore your request. Today, I have accepted the responsibility to become your hand to tell your story, and I will consider it my cross to bear in this life."

My daughter and I immediately began collaboration and we connected on Messenger almost every other day. I shared with her my memories and my reflections of my life's journey. I related my story from its humble beginning to encompass the struggles and lessons learned.

Our spirits connected and aligned. My daughter's gift to inquire into the facts, the history, the emotion with attention to detail and her constant question of why, brought out the deeper meaning of my experiences. Coupled with her gift of storytelling, it stamped the authenticity of this book.

It is my sincere hope that whoever reads my story will receive it with the spirit intended and feel the yearning of my soul to sing the song of God's redeeming love, as I've been enlightened through my journey to discover my life's purpose.

'Uliti Uata
Spring 2022

Chapter 1

The Long Walk

Why Me?

I don't remember my father's face. But, I can still feel my heart beating out of my chest, the adrenaline rushing through my tiny body, hands trembling in fear, sweat running down my forehead, my lungs gasping for air as my eyes welled up with tears. While my four-year-old mind struggled to come to grips with the gravity of this fleeting crisis, the terrible moment was suddenly upon us; silence…as he took his last breath.

However faded this memory has become, the emotions I experienced that day in 1940 are still clear and vivid all these eighty-plus years later.

This moment in time has stood still in my mind as giant and immovable as a boulder, yet as powerful as a tidal wave, constantly forcing its way to the forefront of my thoughts. Although traumatized in recounting this memory, I have no choice but to start here as it sets the course for the rest of my journey. This life-altering situation is pivotal in shaping who I am and understanding the purpose of my life.

The pain of losing a loved one is not just difficult, it is heart-wrenching, and we have yet to find words adequate enough to express such deep and raw emotions. It is not until you've walked a mile in those shoes, feeling that loneliness and experiencing the great void in the lives of those left behind, that one could understand such pain.

Losing my father was earth-shattering and devastating, to say the least. Our loss was further compounded by the fact that we had no piece of land on which to lay him to rest. Feeling lost and abandoned, I silently poured out my soul to God, pleading with Him to please help us.

To say we were destitute would be an understatement. We had no home of our own to return to as we lived with other family members, and the man who put food on the table and clothes on our backs was now gone. Our family had hit rock bottom with no options and no light at the end of the tunnel. Without even a glimpse of better days ahead, we had been swallowed up into misery itself, and we were left with only unanswered questions. I saw despair in my mother's eyes, and the sadness I felt as she cried and hugged my brother, Venisi, and I tightly against her chest is an unforgettable embrace that set about the saga of my life.

When a hospital administrator asked Mother for the funeral details, she broke down.

"Please, oh please, allow me some time to think."

The hospital was in Pangai (the capital of the Ha'apai group of islands), and we lived in Ha'ano, a tiny island on the outskirts of Ha'apai, which was only accessible by boat.

Embarrassed by our family's inability to pay a boat fee to escort Father's body back to Ha'ano, Mother went out to the hospital courtyard to cry, and Venisi and I followed right behind her.

"What to do?" Mother mumbled under her breath, for we had not secured a burial plot for Father. Venisi hugged Mother from behind and cried along with her and kept saying, "I am sorry, Mother, I am so sorry," and I joined in as we clung together for comfort. Mother, left with no choice but to swallow her pride, marched herself to a nearby neighbor. Standing outside of a total stranger's home, she called out, "Malo e lelei, 'oku 'iai ha taha 'i 'apini?" *Hello, is anyone home?*

The head of the Lutui family opened their door and invited us in.

"What brought you to our home?" Mr. Lutui asked.

Mother apologized for the intrusion, introduced herself, then said, "Fakamolemole tangata'eiki, ko si'eku lele mai mo hoku ongo ki'i 'uhiki ke kole atu ha ki'i konga kelekele ke si'i tanu ai hoku husepaniti." *I am sorry for barging in. I have come with my two young sons to ask for a small piece of your land to bury my husband.*

Mr. Lutui, moved by the sincerity of Mother's plea, listened intently. When she finished, he nodded his head as he took pity on us, hearing of our dire situation, and graciously offered a piece of his land for us to use as a burial plot for Father.

Mother was speechless, and the only words she managed to say were, "Malo mu'a si'i 'ofa, koe koloa 'a Tonga koe fakamalo." *Thank you for your love; it is our Tongan treasure to say thank you.*

Then, Mother quickly grabbed my arm on the left and Venisi's arm on the right, and we set out down the dirt road.

"Where to?" I asked.

But there was no response. Just her deep sobs as we walked in silence. Venisi motioned with his finger over his lips to keep quiet. Soon we were sitting on the beach, looking out into the vast ocean with no hope in sight, only emptiness and devastation. Mother broke down and on bended knees, she wailed out in agony a widow's cry.

"Lord, why have Ye deserted us? How are we supposed to continue our lives? Oh, please tell me, how?"

With all the strength she had, she yelled out into the open space of beach, ocean, and sky, releasing her pain and deep sorrow.

Venisi and I watched helplessly in locked arms as he patted my head and said, "'Uliti, it will be okay, little man, but right now, we need to be strong for Mama."

I nodded, then laid my head over his shoulder and whispered, "I trust you, Venisi."

The sun was starting to set, and we felt the cold breeze of the ocean on our faces. Mother finally stood up, dusted off the dirt from her clothing, looked me in the eye and said, "'Uliti, I feel in my heart that you will be the provider for our family."

Mother could see the question marks imprinted all over my blank stare as I was confused and dumbfounded, so she repeated herself. This time, in a cracking yet stern voice, her face swollen and red from crying, she restated what she knew deep in her heart.

"'Uliti, kuo mate ho'omo tamai pea 'oku tau si'i faka'ofa, pea koe falala 'oku 'iho 'aofinima pea moho uma tokotaha pe, keke hoko koe tauhi hotau ki'i famili." *'Uliti, your father has passed away, and I have no choice but to ask you to carry this family on your back, and on your shoulder will be the burden of providing for your older brother and me.*

Venisi immediately concurred and said, "Momma is right, 'Uliti, because you are the smart one, so I agree."

I wanted to ask Mother why, how, and in what universe was this even possible given our current circumstance? But try as I may, I could not even utter a reply because her words cut through me like a sharp-edged sword, imprinting itself on my heart as the weight of the world settled upon my small shoulders. At that very moment, I was transformed from a little four-year-old boy to 'Uliti Uata, the man.

With this new responsibility, I mustered up the courage and asked, "Mother, why me?"

Without missing a beat, she asked, "If not you, then who?" as she knelt and pulled us both into her arms and held onto us for dear life. Mother's embrace was warm as I felt her heartbeat, ba-dum, ba-dum, ba-dum, along with my brother's and mine. A moment of unity, oneness, and a deep connection with each other. All three of our hearts beat in a synchronized rhythm, agreeing unanimously without the need for spoken words.

After some time, Mother wiped off her tears, and with laser focus, her gaze reached my eyes and she said, "'Uliti, you are the only person that can lift us out of poverty, and this is the feeling that has been affirmed to me." She touched my heart. "There is a wise old soul inside of you, 'Uliti. Use it to understand God's purpose for your life. Discover the gift that has been bestowed upon you by the Creator Himself and learn to use your God-given talent to lift us out of this hopeless abyss of reality we are in."

Although I could not fully comprehend what Mother said and all that it meant, my heart accepted this responsibility without understanding the scope of the burden I would have to bear. Little did I know at the time, while looking out into the dark blue ocean, that the sea would become my livelihood and the way to fulfill my destiny. And as wild as my imagination was at the time, nothing could have prepared me for such an undertaking born out of necessity, accepted as a sense of duty, directed by the universe as it obeys commands from a higher source of power.

Venisi picked me up off the ground, swung me around, and yelled out at the top of his lungs, "My baby brother is now all grown up." If Mother's endorsement wasn't enough, Venisi's action certainly nailed my fate, and there was no way to escape but to humbly accept.

Darkness slowly filled the night sky as we headed back to the Niu'ui Hospital. Though only a couple of miles away, this was a long walk as it felt like an eternity because now, we had to deal with the situation at hand, Father's burial.

In Tongan culture, there are customs and traditions of funeral processions that differentiate the classes in our society: royalty, nobles, wealthy, working class, and the poor. We did not fit into any of these categories because even the poor had a place to bury their dead. Our family was considered *koe paea tukuhausia*, absolute destitution and utter despair.

When we reached the hospital, there was no time to grieve. The burial needed to take place first thing the next morning because there was no refrigeration to preserve Father's body. Venisi fetched some water in a small, empty tin can then tidied up the area while I watched him spring into action as though he knew exactly what to do. Mother washed Father's body with utmost care, her touch so very gentle. As she did so, she hummed a common departure hymn sung at Tongan funerals to console the spirit of the dead. This was Mother's way of saying, "Go in peace, my love. We will manage somehow."

Tears flowed uncontrollably down her face as she started to sing the words of the hymn, but she maintained her composure, clearing her throat when her voice became choked with emotion. Then she kissed Father's face with the sweet tenderness of her love and said, "All is well, my love, all is well."

Venisi stroked Father's hair, then pulled me close as Mother hugged us both from behind. Venisi vowed over Father's body that no matter what happened, we would have each other's back and that we would be all right.

The rooster crow sounded as the first sign of daybreak approached. Mother gave us a gentle squeeze. "Come, boys, we have to say our final goodbye to Father." I remember putting my head on his shoulder and said, "Father, I will be good to Mother and Venisi, I promise."

In hindsight, I do not know how Mother pulled us through our darkest hour, for she had buried this moment in time deep into her subconscious mind as an escape to numb the pain. I have often wondered how she found the strength and where she got her tenacity to overcome this painful chapter of her life. One thing I know for sure is a mother's will to protect her children supersedes her own needs and safety. Her instinct, her compassion, and her love were her lifelines that enabled her to say, "This too we shall overcome."

Mother did not consider herself a religious person as she was not a devout Christian and was not a faithful churchgoer, but I beg to differ. She was on a spiritual journey to find God, for she used prayer as a lifeline to communicate to the heavens, seeking answers during the lowest point of her life; why, how, and where do we go from here?

Melepua Finau Uata

Mother had immortalized the stranger that helped us secure a place to lay Father to rest. She constantly reminded Venisi and me never to forget this kindness as she repeatedly asked the Lord for blessings upon the Lutui family. In my young mind, I wanted to be just like the head of this kind family and pay it forward by reaching out and lifting up someone in their time of need. This act of kindness was an inflection point as its lasting effects have been felt for four generations of my family. My heart is overflowing with gratitude and I acknowledge with humility a sincere "Thank you" to the Lutui family, for they removed our shame and allowed us to lift our heads and walk a little taller.

Few books were easily accessible for use at the time, except the bible. One scripture stood out among the rest, for its contents spoke to the core of our experience, written in the Gospel of Matthew, "And Jesus saith unto him, 'The foxes have holes, and the birds of the air have nests; but the Son of man hath not where to lay his head.'" (matthew t. E., 2001)[1]

Over the years, these words brought comfort, eased our pain, gave us hope, and allowed us to have peace in our hearts even in the worst of times.

To this day, I do not know the exact location of my father's grave, but I have come to terms and made peace with it. As I grew older, I found strength in repeating the Serenity Prayer daily:

"God, grant me the serenity to accept the things I cannot change, courage to change the things I can, and wisdom to know the difference." (serenity prayer, 2021)[2]

My father's grave remained unmarked with no tombstone to identify that he once existed in this life. But my relentless search continues to find someone that is still alive to pinpoint the location of his remains so that I can bring him back home and lay him to rest where he belongs.

Father was just an ordinary man who lived a difficult but happy life. He married Sulieti Puafisi (affectionately nicknamed "Melepua"), a woman who loved him dearly and had two sons, Venisi and me. Although I cannot remember his face no matter how hard I try, I have this mental image of a handsome young man with black hair, strong build, fair skin, and big muscles that hoisted me up on his broad shoulders while he happily danced, feeling so proud to have me as his son.

While there is a big void in my life as I still yearn for my father's love, I have accepted God's will. For now, I have secured a place in my heart where my father has been given a proper burial with a grand finale conducted with dignity and honor, along with all the glory thereof as my hero. I imagine a huge gathering of people who would come to pay their respects as he lies in a gold-rimmed coffin draped in white robes, his eulogy read through a loudspeaker for all to hear and for his *hako* offspring to remember. His memory filled with love, his story shared with respect, his name spoken in reverence: "Lisiate Mafi Uata." May his soul rest in peace until we meet again, if only by the grace of God.

Chapter 2

A Boy from Ha'ano

Childhood Years

I finally felt a sense of belonging when we returned to Ha'ano. The view of our island's landmark, Maka-ko-Fele'unga, a stone erected in the sea just outside our shores and right in the

Maka-ko-Fele'unga at Ha'ano, Ha'apai

middle of our tiny island, made my small heart swell with pride. I am not alone in feeling this patriotism, for every Ha'ano person prides themselves in uttering its name. Legend has it that this stone was brought over by a noble person named Vaha'i (A hero from Hihifo, Tongatapu) who was heading back home from Vava'u when he stopped by Ha'ano to rest before he continued with his voyage. He lay down on this rock to rest for the night, and in the morning before he left, released the crabs that he brought, hence the name Maka-ko-Fele'unga, meaning "a stone with crawling crabs."

Saia Finau   Fifita Finau

I left Ha'ano as a little boy, innocent and carefree. But I returned as the appointed patriarch of my family. A man of conviction on that cold, lonely beach, where I vowed that I would provide for my family. To that end, this sense of responsibility changed my perspective of the world.

My maternal grandparents, Saia and Fifita Finau, whom we lived with, welcomed us back with open arms and expressed their condolences for our loss. Mother refused to dwell in their pity. My grandparents tried to find out the details of what happened, but Mother's answer was short and direct: "It is what it is. It is God's will and we have no choice but to accept." I was taken aback by Mother's harsh reply, yet it caused me to ponder on this fate that life had brought upon our family. I delved into a deeper sense of maturity in which my mind shifted into survival mode.

From sunrise to sunset, Mother did all kinds of work. She did everything from weaving mats to pounding tapa cloths for mere pennies on the dollar. Venisi and I were always by her side, helping with daily chores, sweeping, picking up fallen leaves, cooking, and washing clothes by hand. Other days, the three of us went to the sea to *fangota,* catch fish for us to eat. Yet other days, we went and tended to the crops at the *uta,* agricultural land owned by my grandparents, where taro, cassava, sweet potatoes, and bananas were planted. As a bonus, we harvested coconuts where we peeled off their flesh and dried them under the hot sun to be sold. This supplemental income was saved for the sole purpose of school expenses. There was never a moment of rest during the day and by nightfall, my body was so exhausted that I would fall asleep instantly.

Mother made it clear to Venisi that he would not attend school and instead, he would stay behind and work to help her put me through school. I felt sadness just hearing these words and I felt sorry for my brother, but he accepted it wholeheartedly without complaint and always with words of encouragement: "You do us proud, 'Uliti."

I was six when I entered Government Public School (GPS) Ha'ano Elementary School. Mother scraped every penny she had saved to sew me one uniform so I could attend school. My first day was exciting. I woke up early, got myself washed, put on my school uniform, and ran barefoot until I reached the school grounds on an empty stomach. Nothing mattered to me that day. I just wanted to learn, because my mind wanted to absorb anything and everything. When the bell rang, we gathered into the classroom. There were no chairs or desks except a simple mat to cover the dirt floor, but that did not deter my excitement.

However eager I was to learn, my spirit was dampened when I looked around and all the kids took out pencil and paper and I had none. I reminded myself of my motto, "Failure is not an option," but how do I remain optimistic when I lack so much? How do I ask Mother for school supplies when she has none to give?

Different thoughts ran through my mind as I returned home that day, my head slumped downward as I kicked the ground with every step I took. I sat down under the mango tree feeling sorry for myself. I picked up a stick and drew a smiley face on the dirt to help shift my thought process. Suddenly, I heard a man's voice, "'Uliti. 'Uliti."

"Here I am," I answered and as I looked up, it was a neighbor, my first cousin named Vunileva. He handed me a pencil and said, "Use this to make a living."

My heart rejoiced and I jumped up and said, "Hooray! Thank you, Vuni, for this gift. I shall use this pencil wisely." I do not know what prompted my cousin to offer me the pencil, but I am sure he figured out that I needed one. To me, I took his action as heaven's way of saying it will be all right, son. Everything will be okay.

I ran toward our *fale pola* (a small Tongan hut, round in shape, composed of freshly woven coconut branches) holding the pencil in my hand and yelled out, "Melepua! Venisi! Look! Vuni just gave me this pencil for school." We were all so grateful because even a gift as simple as this pencil made a significant difference in my life. It boosted my confidence with endless possibilities of hope. Instead of focusing on what I lacked, the pencil represented a better tomorrow.

After about a month, it became apparent that I was a smart and bright child. By the end of the first quarter, the teacher told Mother that I was too advanced in my studies to remain at Ha'ano. Mother, staying true to her conviction, called a family meeting. "'Uliti," she said, "I will send you to Pangai to live with my sister Suli and her family so you can attend a better school."

Stunned, I stormed out toward the open fields and cried by myself, not wanting to be separated from my family. The feeling of abandonment was surreal, and I did not want to accept it. Soon, my brother came around the corner and gave me a chokehold. "Stop crying, you little tweet," he teased while he ruffled my hair.

I snapped back, "Easy for you to say because you will stay behind with Mother while I will be sent away." Venisi tried his best to comfort me, but nothing was registering in my head.

"Come on now, little man, you know that if I could switch places with you, I would in a heartbeat. But we both know that only you can fulfill this huge responsibility riding on your shoulders to provide for our little family." He continued, "It is your destiny, 'Uliti, so stop fighting the path Mother laid out for you."

By this time, I had calmed down and stopped crying, then looked up and asked, "Venisi, why are you willing to forgo school because of me?"

He simply answered, "Because you are gifted with a smart brain, and I am so proud of you." This was the first heart-to-heart talk I had with my brother, and his words made me feel safe under his wing.

I interrupted this intimate moment as I ran back home teasing my brother, "Na na nana na. You can't make me."

Venisi was furious as he ran after me saying, "'Uliti, stop, or I swear I will beat you up."

I replied, "Well, you need to catch me first," and I continued running until I was out of breath.

Venisi caught up and tackled me to the ground right outside our *fale pola*. "I dare you to say it again. Say it again, you little punk."

Mother stormed outside and said, "Boys, stop it right now. Our family's future is at stake and you are messing around like that?" We both immediately sat down on the ground as Mother tried to sweet talk me into changing my mind, but I was stubborn and remained steadfast in my decision not to go.

"You have left me with no choice," Mother said as she grabbed a stick and beat me to my senses. But no matter how hard she hit, I did not shed a tear. With every stroke of the stick she asked, "Have you had enough?" and I yelled out the answer in my mind, "No, not even close." She continued until the stick broke and she exhausted herself. As Mother slumped down to the ground, she said, "'Uliti, do you think it is easy for me to send you away?"

I could not answer because in the Tongan culture, it is impolite and disrespectful to talk back to your parents, so I gently answered her question, "Yes, I do," and before I could finish justifying the answer in my mind, she said, "No mother wants to be separated from her child, but sacrifices are necessary." Mother continued, "I want to send you to a better school because you are smart. Don't you get it?"

By this time Mother was sobbing as Venisi tried to comfort her, but she pushed him away as she inched herself closer to me. "'Uliti," she said, "I know it is difficult for you to leave, but remember what I have always said: "Only through an education can you lift us out of poverty." My brain knew what Mother said was right, but my heart refused to accept it.

As days went by, I saw the sadness on Mother's face and I tried to cheer her up, but nothing worked. She looked as though every ounce of energy had drained out from her body and I said, "I am sorry, Mother."

She replied, "It is okay, son. I understand how you feel and I cannot make you do anything against your will." Days turned into weeks and weeks turned into months as the three of us experienced frequent awkward silences that started to wear me down. Finally, I decided to get over this silly, childish tantrum and get on with the business of what I was meant to do, because I could not bear to see Mother depressed. One day as Mother hovered over the open fire cooking our evening meal, I hugged her from behind and said, "I am sorry, Mother, for upsetting you. Please forgive me and I will go to Pangai for school."

She turned around, held up my face toward hers, and said, "Thank you, my son. Thank you, 'Uliti, for accepting this pathway you are destined to walk."

This was exceedingly difficult and a painful crossroad I came to at this point in my life, yet it was a necessary path I needed to cross. I decided in my young mind not to dwell on what lay ahead and just focus on this moment. Enjoy the time I had left with my family because I was not sure if or when I would be back to see them again.

I remember it was near Christmastime and Grandpa Saia told us boys to go and *ta'aki manioke*, dig up cassava roots from the *'uta* and bring taro leaves for our Sunday meal. It was a sizzling summer day and I didn't want to go, so I whined and complained. "I want to go swimming," I mumbled to Venisi. "I just want to have fun with you before I leave for school."

He squatted down and said, "We can still have fun, little man. Come on. I will give you a piggyback ride if you stop complaining."

I jumped on his back and said, "Giddyap, let's go," and Venisi ran as I tapped my feet on his sides like I was riding a horse.

As we approached our *'uta*, we saw a figure from a distance, and as we got closer, we realized he was Grandpa's brother Peni digging up cassava roots from our plantation. We immediately turned around and ran home without stopping. We saw Mother on our way and she asked, "Why are you boys running, and why are you coming back emptyhanded?"

We both tried to catch our breaths and Venisi said, "Mother, you would not believe what we just witnessed."

Mother laughed it off and asked, "What did you boys see, a ghost?"

"No, Mother," Venisi continued. "Do not be alarmed, but your uncle Peni is stealing cassava from our field right now, and I need to hurry and tell Grandpa."

Mother said, "That is okay. He is just getting food for his family to eat."

"What do you mean?" Venisi demanded an answer and I concurred.

Mother calmly said, "I can see there are things I need to pass on to you as it was taught to me. Come along, boys." Mother pulled us both by the hand. "We need to talk."

I realized we were heading to the beach instead of home and I asked, "Mother, aren't we going in the wrong direction?" and she replied, "I want us to talk privately so Grandpa will not hear our conversation."

I thought to myself, "This is strange. Why would Mother not want Grandpa to hear us talk? After all, it is his *'uta*. He should be aware that someone has been stealing from him. And his brother, of all people."

My curiosity soon ended as we reached the beach. We sat down on the hot sand under the shade of a tree branch, then Mother said, "Boys, I want you to listen very carefully to what I am about to tell you." We were attentive as she continued, "The man you saw in our plantation field today is family and he is not stealing from us. He was digging up food to feed his own family."

Venisi interrupted and asked, "Mother, I am sorry. I do not mean to talk back and be disrespectful, but you have always taught us not to steal, so why are you justifying your uncle's actions when we caught him red-handed?"

Mother answered with a hushed tone, "When a family member comes to take something of ours, that is not stealing. He is simply trying to feed his family." She continued, "For example, Venisi, if you had a plantation field and someone comes to tell you that they saw your brother 'Uliti digging up food from your land, would you consider that stealing?"

Venisi quickly said, "Of course not."

Mother asked, "Why not?"

"Because he is my brother," replied Venisi.

Mother took both our hands and held them together close to her heart. "You see, boys, if you go and tell Grandpa, he will tell you the same thing as I am telling you now because this is what he taught me when I was a little girl. Family is family and that is that."

Venisi and I looked at each other as we came to this realization that the bond Grandpa and his brother had was too deep for us to invade. We just received a life lesson from this experience, and it made me realize the depth of my feelings toward my brother. I cannot even explain it, but it is there, solid and firm. Mother told us to go swimming, then get the cassava afterward. "Yes, ma'am. You do not have to tell us twice." Then off we ran and jumped into the water. We both swam toward *Maka-ko-Fele'unga* and joined the others already there. We were just being kids. I climbed onto Venisi's shoulders as we played water wrestling with the other boys, and we had so much fun with no worries of the world.

The day of our departure, Mother and Venisi woke up in the wee hours of the morning and made *umu*, a ground oven, and baked *manioke,* cassava. This type of cooking is reserved only for a Sunday meal, which is considered a special meal. She wrapped them in a taro leaf and handed them to me saying, "Koe fo'i manioke paku ena keke 'oho," *Here are some burned cassava for you to eat on your journey.* Mother then handed me a letter with a *fakapona*, a piece of clothing that money is wrapped tightly in, and gave specific instructions. "You give this to your Auntie Suli when you arrive at Pangai." I said my goodbyes to Grandma and Grandpa then off we went down to the waters.

Students departing from Ha'ano to Pangai for school was a huge yearly event. The whole island came out to the beach to say their goodbyes. There were only three students all together including myself, but we were honored that day as though we did something extraordinary, leaving our homeland for school. Mother, Venisi, and I hugged each other like there was no tomorrow as I sobbed uncontrollably. After a while, Mother wiped the tears off my face and let my hands go saying, "It is time, 'Uliti. Have a safe journey."

Everyone cried when we hopped onto the small boat, and as we waved goodbye, they yelled out, "Boys, remember, do not look back. Only focus on school." Another yelled out, "Stay the course and do not give up," and another said, "When you leave, do not come back unless you bring an addition to Ha'ano." Their voices echoed the message, "Do not look back and do Ha'ano proud." Feeling overwhelmed as tears streamed down my face, I experienced an "aha" moment. At such an early age, I represented hope. *School is the pathway to freedom and I carry the whole island's dreams on my shoulders.* The atmosphere of patriotism and loyalty filled the air as love and care were felt throughout this tight community, and this had been my resolve to study hard at school then return and give back to the people of my hometown.

As we drifted off into the open sea, I looked back and could still make out figures in the far distance, but what stood out to me the most was Mother's white handkerchief still waving until it was out of sight. My heart sank as I covered my eyes and sobbed quietly. Even at the tender age of seven, when the world around me had not all made sense yet, this emotion was so deep and raw that words cannot fully express it.

The boat rocked back and forth as I pulled out the *manioke paku*, burned cassava Mother made, and it was as sweet as candy as I slowly chewed on it. I then dipped it into the salty seawater and took another bite. It was the juiciest thing I had ever eaten, and I savored every bite. I used every sense of my body to remember this experience and recorded this day in my memory bank. I closed my eyes and made this silent vow: *I know not what tomorrow will bring, but if education is truly my family's road to financial freedom, then come what may, I shall endure.*

Chapter 3

Unchartered Territory

Leaving Home in Search of an Education

We arrived in Pangai, a daunting new place of uncharted territory, yet one that represented hope. As we got off the boat, families lined up to greet the other boys, and I looked around to see if I could recognize my auntie but quickly realized that no one came for me. It was an unwelcoming feeling, but I rationalized that I had encountered much worse situations. I grabbed my bag and said goodbye to my friends then headed out. I asked around for directions to my auntie's house and all the while kept repeating Mother's words in my mind, *It is what it is*, and I had no time to dwell on self-pity. Soon, I found myself outside Auntie Suli's house. "Who is it?" someone asked.

"I am looking for Suli Talakai's house?"

"Yes," came the answer, and she said, "Who is asking?"

Unsure of what to say, I simply handed her the letter Mother gave me, and the *fakapona*.

Auntie Suli hugged me and said, "Come in, child. Come in. Here, sit down. Wow, you have grown up quite a bit, 'Uliti, from the last time I saw you." I looked at her face, but I did not recall ever meeting her. "Tell me about my sister. How is she doing?" My face lit up as I spoke Mother's name. I gave her an update on everyone back home, including Venisi, Grandma Fifita, and Grandpa Saia.

"Oh, I have missed them so much," Suli continued, "but I cannot believe my sister sent you here all by yourself. You pitiful thing."

"It is okay," I replied, "Mother told me I must be strong." Suli hugged me again as she called her husband and her children to come and meet me.

The greeting was very informal because in the Tongan culture, when a family member, either close or extended, is present, they are considered to be "home," and they are always welcome. Auntie Suli said to everyone, "My nephew will be staying with us for school for a couple of years until he is ready for high school, then he will be leaving for Tongatapu. In the meantime, he will be an extension to our family." She turned toward me and said, "'Uliti, we don't have much to offer you."

To which I quickly replied, "You don't have to explain, Suli, I understand."

"Well then, young man, if you say so," came her response. I nodded my head in agreement and tried to express my heartfelt gratitude for Auntie's kindness, but all I was able to manage was a quiet thank you. Although I knew I was an outsider to Auntie's family, her words were comforting and helped calm my nerves.

There was not enough room for all of us to fit in their home, so Auntie Suli and her husband, Kelepi, made an extension to their house called a *fakafaletolo*. It's like a tent with a roof and a wall, meant for me to sleep in. At

Suli & Kelepi Talakai

night, they would close their door, and I slept in this tent, quaking with fear as I recalled many ghost stories and legends I'd heard Venisi and the other boys tell back home. But through it all, I was so grateful to them for their kindness in putting a roof over my head.

We were given daily chores and they had to be done regardless. No excuses and no exceptions. I was assigned a specific responsibility, and that was to *hiki ee hoosi* (reposition the horse to a better grass area for food). I did this in the morning before I went to school as well as in the afternoon when I returned from school.

Siope Talakai

Auntie Suli had a son named Siope Talakai, a very handsome boy, and he was their *fo'i pele* (like the prince of the family) where he did not do any work and his chores were reassigned to me instead. Everything from making the *haka* (our daily meals) to cleaning and washing and going to the *uta* on the weekend to help my uncle with plantation work. But I did not complain. I was just grateful to Auntie and her family for taking me in.

Occasionally, Suli would say, "'Uliti, Melepua sent me some money." When I inquired on how she obtained the money, she explained, "Your mother and brother went by boat to 'Uiha (a neighboring island from Ha'ano) and that is where Grandpa Saia is from. They went to Grandpa's family and asked if they could *fua niu* (collect coconuts) from their land, peel the flesh, dry them under the sun, pack them up in bags, and sell them by the pound." The money from this work was sent to Suli to help with my school expenses.

I was so touched to know that they did that for me, but at the same time, I was saddened to hear how much work they had to do just to keep me in school. These were the thoughts that kept me focused on school as I imagined the arduous work Mother and Venisi must do just to send spare change to help support my education. I came to accept this reality as I endured all sorts of mistreatments from Suli's family because I could not bear the thought that I would be a disappointment to Mother and Venisi.

The new school year was a big event for families, in anticipation of buying new uniforms and school supplies, but I knew better than to expect anything. My auntie's family was no exception, even when money was tight. The new school year was just around the corner and Mother did not send any money for my school expenses.

I recall vividly as I lay outside in the tent, hearing my auntie and uncle discuss uniforms and school supplies for their kids. I heard Taisia, Auntie Suli's oldest daughter, say to her parents, "'Oua mu'a na'a si'i ngalo 'a 'Uliti ke 'ai hano vala ako mo ha'ane naunau ako." *Please don't forget 'Uliti and get him a uniform and school supplies.* Taisia's sweet words became my pillar of strength because I felt her love as she advocated on my behalf. Her kindness and her care made me feel like I belonged. That human connection was what I was longing for as I craved acceptance from Auntie Suli's family. I lay awake that night as tears welled up in my eyes and I said in my mind, *Thank you, Taisia. I shall treasure your words forever, and in a moment I needed it most.* And with that grateful thought, I dozed off to sleep.

Taisia Folau

This single incident left a huge impression in my mind and impacted my life. It shifted my attitude and my perception. It reminded me of the vow I made on the day I arrived at Pangai. Come what may, I shall endure. I found solace in Taisia's kind words, which penetrated my heart and gave me strength to stay the course and carry on.

As days turned into weeks and weeks turned into months and months turned into years, the chores became so burdensome due to pure exhaustion from doing them day in and day out. I remember it was a rainy day and I had just returned from repositioning the horse and it was dark and dreary outside. Instead of telling me to come in and change my clothes, one of my cousins said, "'Uliti, you cannot come in until you make the *haka*. I was shivering in wet clothes as I turned toward our *peito* (outside kitchen).

I started to build a fire while I peeled off the taro skin then filled up the *kulo* (pot) with water. Soon after, I heard someone calling to check when the *haka* would be ready, but I did not reply. I sat by the fire and warmed myself up, but my anger was stirring inside. Finally, I about had it, so I stood up and deliberately dropped the pot to the ground. My auntie ran out, saw what had happened, and she gave me a beating. And instead of feeling the pain, I felt proud of my actions.

We all went without food that evening and I felt liberated. In a moment of defiance, I finally had the courage to silently act a bit rebellious in hopes that they would stop *pu'i* (asking me to do chores) as my young body was too exhausted.

I was in fourth grade when one day, Mother made a surprise visit. I saw her figure from a distance and I dropped the coconut I was holding and ran toward her. I hugged her and cried, asking, "Mother, why has it taken you so long to visit me?"

She simply said, "I am sorry, son, but I'm here now." I continued crying as I tried to explain in between sobs how I had been mistreated. She held her hand over my mouth so her sister would not hear. She took me to the wharf, then finally released her hand and said, "Cry, 'Uliti. Cry as much as you want, son, then tell me all about it." I explained in detail how badly I had been treated, then begged Mother to please take me back to Ha'ano with her. She wiped my tears dry and said, "There, there, my son, I hope you feel better now." I nodded my head, then Mother gave me an update on how things were going back home with my brother and grandparents.

Now my sad face turned into a smile. She knelt to eye level, held my face, and with the most loving voice, she said, "'Uliti, I will not take you back to Ha'ano because there is nothing there for you." She continued, "I want you to be my strong little man and stay the course. I am sorry, but you must endure all the hardships you face because sacrifices are deemed necessary at this time for the future of our family."

My heart-to-heart talk with Mother soothed my mind and my energy was renewed. She took out a small basket woven with coconut leaves and inside was food made for me. It had *manioke paku* and *lu ika* (fish in coconut milk wrapped in taro leaves). "Oh, what a treat!" I exclaimed. "Thank you, Mother." The food satisfied my hunger, and it was the most delicious meal I had tasted simply because it was made with a mother's love. Sadly enough, I had to say goodbye to Mother yet again, but I reminded myself of my destiny as Mother believed in it wholeheartedly and I believed it myself. I swallowed my sorrow and accepted my fate.

Another two years had passed and I was now in sixth grade. As the school year ended, then came the big event. This was when an entrance exam was given to all primary school students to determine which high school they could be admitted to. The number-one school that everyone aimed to get into was Tonga High School, and only the best and brightest with the highest score marks could enter. This was such a prestigious recognition, not just for the student but for their family and the village or island the student was from, for it brought great honor for the whole community.

I studied hard for this test because I wanted to make Mother and Venisi proud, for I knew they would be all ears to learn of the outcome. The exam day arrived and I was nervous yet determined. The test itself was not difficult, but the pressure I had put on myself felt overwhelming. My palms were sweaty as I wrote down my answers, and I kept repeating to myself, "I will pass. I will succeed. Failure is not an option."

It took a couple of weeks for the results to be received by our school principal as we anxiously waited to hear the news. Finally, the day came and the test results were announced. We had a school assembly and the principal started to announce the names of each student and which school they could attend. Finally, I heard him say, "'Uliti Uata from Ha'ano, Ha'apai—Pass to Tonga High School."

I remained calm and maintained my composure until school was over. As soon as the bell rang, I ran to the shores, looked out into the ocean, and yelled out, "Mother, Venisi, did you hear the good news?! I did it, and it is all thanks to your support!" My joy overflowed as I jumped up and down and said, "Whoop, whoop! A Ha'ano boy passed to Tonga High School." It was silly, of course, because I knew they could not hear me, yet I felt such a deep connection to them that even though we were miles and miles apart, we all felt the joy of that moment and we celebrated it in our hearts.

Instead of returning home, I walked to the Niu'ui Hospital and tried to locate Father's burial plot outside its courtyard. I looked and I looked but I just could not remember. Everything was foggy in my memory. The only thing I remembered was that we dug a hole in the ground and buried Father's body, but there was no marking to identify his burial plot.

Nighttime was quickly approaching and I had to leave before it became dark. I slowly walked the path heading back home, feeling sad that I did not get to share my moment of joy with Father. I saw a *tava* tree (lychee tree) and I sat down next to its trunk and said a silent prayer, hoping it would reach the heavens, and asked, "Father, are you there? I hope you are looking down and watching me from above. I just came to share the good news with you that I passed the exam to Tonga High School. You are proud of me, right?" But of course, there was no answer except sounds of nature.

A couple of weeks later, the school principal approached me and said, "'Uliti, you did great on the exam and you passed with an exceedingly high score. I am immensely proud of you; however, Tonga High School cannot accept you because you are too old. You have surpassed the acceptance age."

Talk about bursting bubbles. His words dropped me from a high elevation of pure joy and smashed me right down to the ground. "What can I do?" I asked. His only answer was to attend my second school of choice. My short lived excitement was crushed. Mother's word, *it is what it is*, allowed me to accept this fact with grace. My heart sank, and with downcast eyes, I apologized quietly in my mind. "I am sorry, Mother and Venisi, for being a disappointment." It occurred to me that what I felt was self-pity, so my mind quickly reverted to what Mother had said, "It is what it is," and so I swallowed this bitter news and accepted it not as a failure but as an obstacle to overcome.

Although I could not attend the most prestigious school that everyone wanted access to due to their admission policy, I was still excited knowing that I passed with flying colors. About six months afterward, Mother and Venisi came with my boat fee to Tongatapu. The day of their arrival at Pangai, I saw a sense of pride on their faces. My brother lifted me off the ground as he hugged me and said, "I knew you could do it, 'Uliti. I just knew it."

Mother nodded in agreement then said, "I knew it from the beginning. I don't know how, but I knew in my heart 'Uliti is a smart boy and will do amazing things."

I remember that day like it was just yesterday. The flowers were in full bloom, and walking to the wharf I saw birds of paradise, frangipani, allamanda, and hibiscus growing wild in the fields. The fragrance of the *siale* (gardenia) and the *pua tonga* (gardenia taitensis) filled the air with its intoxicating aroma. The clear blue sky could be seen for miles, the sun was out, and the ocean breeze blew ever so softly upon our faces. Mother and Venisi were on each of my sides holding my hands tightly.

I savored this moment in time. I treasured this memory, for it was the first time I felt whole, that I was somebody's son, someone's brother. This invigorating feeling of happiness, even if it was just for a day, freed me of the pain I had carried and confirmed in my mind that I was destined to do great things. I was fourteen at the time and I knew that I had to man up and accept my destiny as the provider for our little family, which was a great responsibility.

Chapter 4

Forward and Onward

Quest for a Better Tomorrow

Mother's last words to me before we parted came in a whispered tone, and she basically shared the same message as when I left Ha'ano seven years earlier: "'Uliti, when you leave to Tongatapu, do not look back and do not come back."

I asked her, "Why not? I want to come back."

She said, "You need only to stay focused with your schooling, then find a woman to be an extension of our Ha'ano family."

I lifted my eyes to meet hers and I said, "Yes, Mother. I shall do that."

"No tears now, young man. Do you hear me? And do not look back." I took a deep breath, then exhaled slowly as I nodded my head.

Auntie Suli escorted me on this trip to make necessary arrangements for housing. I felt so proud when I handed over my passenger pass to the ticket agent as I entered the MV *Hifofua*, the boat that would take me to my destiny. I sat on the deck so I could have a full view of the Ha'apai Islands, and I took a mental picture and cemented it in my memory forever. I heard both my mother and brother yelling, "Goodbye, 'Uliti! And remember, do not come back. We will come to you." I waved goodbye but my head did not turn around as I focused forward and onward on the journey to my destination, Tongatapu.

The boat ride was rough but manageable. I felt nauseous and my tummy was uneasy. I put my head over the side of the boat and tried to vomit but nothing came out. Auntie Suli put one hand over my head and rubbed my back with the other to help me feel better as the boat floated over the open sea. My curiosity deepened on how a boat could withstand such a beating from the ocean and manage to stay afloat.

Although I felt sick to my stomach, I could not help my fascination with the dark blue color of the deep ocean, the sounds of the waves crashing against the boat, and the fierce power it had to lift up the boat like a lifeless piece of wood, then slam it back down, then up again and down again. Wow. The ocean truly has its own majestic aura as an unmatched force of nature to be respected.

My attention turned to the sound of folk songs (*hiva kakala*) sung by the passengers to ride out the long journey. Soon after, they switched to gospel music and oh, these strangers' voices harmonized like an a cappella choir. I closed my eyes, tapping my foot to its rhythm as I felt this reverent energy echoing in the air.

'Eiki ko e 'ofa 'a'au, koe moana loloto
(Lord, thy love is as deep as the ocean)

Pea ngalo hifo kiai, 'eku ngaahi angahia
(And my sins are drowned in the depths thereof)
Pea kuo 'ufi'ufi 'eku kovi kotoa pe
(And Ye covered up all my sins)
'Eku kovi kotoa pe
(Covered up all my sins)

'I he vaivai hoku sino, pea vaivai moe loto
(When my body is weak, my heart is too)
'E poupou 'e he taulani hoku laumalie holi
(My connection to thee supports my yearning soul)
Pea u ongo'i 'o 'ilo 'ae 'ofa ta'engata
(And I feel and know thy everlasting love)
'Ae 'ofa ta'engata
(Thy everlasting love)
(KO E TOHI HIMI (SIASI UESILIANA TAU'ATAINA 'O TONGA, n.d.)³

What is this feeling that I am experiencing? I asked myself. For I felt like I was floating on cloud nine as the sound of this music penetrated my soul and its words resonated in my heart. I had known for some time a special connection to a higher source of power, but this emotion moved me as I sang along with others giving praises to God with gratitude beyond expression. I bowed my head and said a silent prayer: "Thank you. Thank you." Then I went back up to the deck and lay flat on my back.

I looked up, and gazed upon the brightness of the stars while opening my arms to embrace the ocean wind gusting across the boat. Soon someone called out, "I can see light," and handclaps erupted among the passengers with one after another saying, "'Aue, malo kuo tau fonua si'etau folau." (*Oh thank goodness, our journey has seen land.*)

Then another passenger with a loud voice said, "Let us pray." He read out each verse of a hymn where everyone joined in and sang along. He then offered a somber prayer of gratitude, thanking the Lord for our safe journey, and at the end, everyone sang *The Lord's Prayer* then ended with 'Emeni. 'Emeni. (*Amen. Amen.*)

As we embarked from the Hifofua to the Uafu Vuna (Vuna Wharf), I stood on the soil of Tongatapu and thought to myself, there is no turning back now.

No one came to greet us at the wharf, but I expected that much. Auntie Suli and I walked to Kolomotu'a, a city within the suburb of the capital, Nuku'alofa, to find the home of Misitana Vea. The only thing I knew was that this was a relative of Auntie Suli's husband, and if you have family who live in Tongatapu, you are considered lucky. The connection of family ties is the fabric that weaves a closeknit feeling of community, a sense of belonging, and is the fundamental root of our culture. For our culture does not allow anyone to be homeless, no matter how poor we are as a country. All Tongans are taught this principle concept to share food, clothing, and shelter with one another.

Misitana & Meleseini Vea

Auntie Suli introduced me to the family and simply said, "I'm going back to Ha'apai, but I will leave my nephew 'Uliti in your care so he can attend school." A mutual agreement was reached and the Vea family was kind to me and provided housing and food if they had any leftovers, but that was the extent of their help.

I was left to fend for myself and figure things out on my own for Mother and Venisi could not help me simply because we were too poor. In 1950, I got myself registered at Liahona High School. I was only able to attend one term as I had no choice but to drop out because I could not afford to pay the school fees. I registered in other high schools such as 'Atele, Saint Andrews, and 'Apifo'ou, and I used the same tactics—dropped out after one term when the tuition must be paid. Due to the limited number of schools in Tongatapu, I reached the end of my school-hopping days, but I enjoyed its privileges while it lasted.

I went back to Liahona because at this time, the school principal was Loiti Talakai (nicknamed La'iafi) and he was Auntie Suli's husband Kelepi's son before they were married. He allowed me to attend school while I worked to pay for my school fees.

Loiti Talakai

I was treated kindly by others because I was known as the principal's brother. During this time, Liahona was a newly formed school. The classrooms consisted of several *fale Tonga* (a traditional Tongan thatched-roof house, rectangular in shape with sides made of woven coconut leaves). When it rained, the water came into the classroom and we had to end school until it receded and the ground dried up again.

Construction was underway to modernize the school, and Mr. Motoni was now Liahona's school principal. I had no way to pay for my school tuition, so I approached him with a proposal. He was gracious enough to allow me to work on the construction project after school and on the weekends, and my labor paid for my school tuition.

Mr. Emili—Mission Pres & Head Church Construction

Mr. Emili was both mission president and head of all the church construction projects. Each division was led by a foreigner, but they used local laborers. School students also helped, so we would attend school one day then work the next day. This alternation of school and workdays went on from Monday through Friday. I remember there were two trucks, a Ford and a Bedford. There was a generator and a stone drill machine. The construction was completed around 1953 or 1954 and the school was a beautiful sight to behold. The president of The Church of Jesus Christ of Latter-Day Saints at the time, President David O. McKay, flew to Tonga and officially opened the new, modernized Liahona High School.

Sione Tu'alau Latu

Viliami Sika

I met some of my closest and dearest friends at Liahona—Sione Tu'alau Latu, Loni 'Unga Sikahema, Viliami Sika, Palauni Fine, Kauasi Mataele, Sione 'Akauola Havea, Siope Havea, Heneli Vea, Semisi Palavi Kioa, and Tevita Tautua'a. Of course, there were many other friends, but I had such a close relationship with these young men, and I considered them my closest circle of friends. However, there were six of us that bonded like magnets because of our similar family situations.

We each had our own struggles and we all came from a poor background with no family support, so we turned to each other for help. Among us were Loni 'Unga Sikahema, Tevita Tautua'a, Semisi Palavi Kioa, Siope Havea, and Heneli Vea. We had one school uniform to share and we had a nonverbal agreement that one would wear the uniform and attend school while the rest of us stayed behind and pretended to be sick. After school, the person who wore the uniform would wash it that evening and hang it to dry for the next day.

The process repeated, one of us would wear the uniform and attend school while the rest stayed behind. But the caveat was that whoever reached the clothesline first and grabbed the uniform would be the person attending school. So we would often race with each other, trying to grab the uniform, and we made do with what we had at the time. This is how we survived high school, by the grace of good friends.

One such friend was my mortal enemy at the beginning but later became one of my closest and dearest friends. Semisi Palavi Kioa was a *matapule* (a teacher's aide) and the rules were, when the *matapule* blows the whistle for the first time, everyone gets up and gets ready. Second time the *matapule* blows the whistle, everyone stands in line and gets ready to *huo* (dig and clear fields in the plantation). Every time Semisi blew the whistle right outside our dorm room door, he asked, "'Uliti, why are you not getting up?" And I replied, "Just write me up and I will be punished with manual labor (*ngaue mo'ua*) later but for right now, I just need a little bit more sleep." We rubbed each other the wrong way because Semisi saw me as a threat challenging his authority, and I saw him as a bully. But as time went by, he was curious as to what made me so bold to stand up to him, and I was curious as to why he was mean and always picked on me.

Our curiosity got the best of us and we started talking, probing, and asking questions. We began to see each other in a different light as we held intimate conversations about our families and learned that our similarities far outweighed our differences. Because of this shift in attitude, whenever Semisi had food, he would always share with me, and, slowly but surely, we developed a close friendship bond that connected us like brothers.

When the school term ended, most of my friends and I stayed behind at the dorm for two reasons. One was out of consideration not to burden the extended family that helped house us. And second, we took advantage of this opportunity to work ahead to pay for our school fees and got free meals, which was always a plus. We milked cows, helped in the plantation field, and worked to keep up school grounds. If we were lucky, we worked for Siale Round, a *hafekasi palangi* (half-Tongan and half-Caucasian), and we used that extra money to help buy school supplies and clothes. Our friendship deepened because we understood each other's struggle, shared each other's pain, and turned toward each other for comfort.

My mind absorbed information like a sponge as I hungered for knowledge. As soon as I learn an innovative idea, I work it out mentally by putting pieces together until a complete picture forms in my mind. I challenged myself with this learning method to gain a better understanding of what was being taught. I didn't just want to be book smart, but used the knowledge I gained and applied it to real-life situations. If we were cited at school for misbehaving, we would *ngaue mo'ua* (be punished to work) after school. I always took my books with me and studied while I was working in detention. Even though I missed a lot of school days, I usually ended up with the highest score on the exam.

I remember one year during the *tanaki tu'unga* (annual class announcement assembly), I took the number-one spot, and the second spot went to a girl named Haisini 'Ulufonua. As she went up to get her *pale* (recognition gift), she cried because she thought she

Vaha'i Tonga

would come out first. Unsatisfied with the result, she launched a formal complaint to our teacher, Vaha'i Tonga, to investigate the exam because she felt it was rigged. Vaha'i responded with confidence, "I am not surprised that this boy took the number-one spot because he is from Ha'ano. If he was from another island, I would investigate further, but Ha'ano has a reputation of producing smart kids." I felt proud as I quietly celebrated each milestone I reached, each hurdle I jumped, and each bridge I crossed. Even if they were small victories, each pushed me forward with my commitments.

In 1955, my mother, Melepua, and Venisi managed to save enough money and they finally came to Tongatapu. Oh what joy that our little family was finally reunited again after six long years of separation. We lived with Mother's family in Kolonga, a village located on the northeast coast of Tongatapu in the Hahake District, a hereditary estate of Lord Nuku. There Melepua met this genuinely nice gentleman named Hiko and shortly thereafter they were married, in 1956.

It was my senior year at Liahona and the distance between Kolonga and Liahona is roughly fifteen miles to my best estimate. On Sundays, students who lived in the dorm showed off as family members dropped off *me'akai Sapate* (Sunday meal) for them to eat and share with friends. I had never experienced such an honor, nor did I come to expect it as I knew full well the long distance, not to mention the lack of transportation.

One Sunday afternoon, I was by myself reading a book under a coconut tree to escape the long scorching summer day. I heard my name being called from afar off, "'Uliti, where are you?" I replied, "Here I am," and came running to see who was calling. As I came around the corner, I saw my stepfather, Hiko, on a bicycle all sweaty and holding a basket woven with coconut leaves. Surprised, I asked, "How? Why did you have to come this far, Hiko?" He smiled and handed me the basket of my *me'akai Sapate* and said, "You silly goose. I came on my bicycle to give you your Sunday meal that your mother made."

I opened with excitement and it had *lu ika* (fish meat in coconut milk wrapped in taro leaves), *manioke paku* (burned cassava), *lo'i lesi* (papaya porridge), and *to'okutu* (a Tongan treat made of flour mixed with water and coconut flakes, sweetened with sugar, and baked in a ground oven in a coconut shell). I felt honored and I felt loved. With gratitude bundled up inside, I said, "Thank you, Hiko. I shall enjoy this food." He replied, "Don't forget to share with your friends," as he hopped back on his bicycle and headed back home. Now I understood why families would travel long distances to give us students food. It was their way of saying, "We love you. Cheer up. The whole family is proud of you."

Graduation day finally arrived in 1957 as I turned twenty-one. My schoolmates and their families celebrated this big event as a huge milestone in their lives, while I saw it as the beginning of my future. The fear of the unknown occupied my thoughts. Overwhelmed with uncertainty, I turned inward and did a self-talk, with me, myself, and I. The challenging questions lay before me. What is next? Where do I go from here? How do I use my education to make a living and support my family?

The harsh reality hit me like a ton of bricks. More than ninety percent of the Tongan male population made their living by fishing and agriculture, and women by weaving mats and making tapa cloths. Only a very small percentage worked for the government and the private sector earning below acceptable wage.

When I weighed out this unbalanced scale in my mind, I knew that I must create a new path for myself. The answer was clear and obvious: to start a business. I reasoned, that is the only way I can be the provider for my family and help the people of Ha'ano. But how do I even start when I have no business model? What resources do I have available at my disposal? Trying to figure out answers to these hard questions overwhelmed my mind. Even sleep became a burden as this riddle filled my every waking thought for months on end.

Consumed by this dream of running a business, I felt the ocean calling for me. Soon I found myself in front of the seashore. A place of refuge and solace as it became sacred ground where I escaped into a dream world. I would look out at the open sea and focus on its horizon as the sun was setting. This view took me back in my memory as Mother's words rang in my ear like thunder: "Your father has passed away and I have no choice but to ask you to carry this family on your back." I wanted to deafen the sound so I closed my eyes, quieted my mind, and meditated.

    Peace began to fill my heart as my creative mind flashed pictures across my mind of my imaginary world. It was serene and lush with coconut trees surrounding the area as I stood in the middle of this beautiful meadow and bathed in the warmth of the sun. A breeze ever so lightly and gently blew across my face. Minutes turned into hours as I had this big grin on my face while envisioning this made-up universe, as I escaped my harsh reality, even if only in my mind.

Chapter 5

Humble Beginning

Birth of the Uata Family

I landed my first job with the Marine Department in 1958 since I passed the government exam, *sivi tutuku 'ae pule'anga,* while at Liahona. And at this time, the finance, post office, and the marine departments were all under the leadership of the Minister of Finance, and my direct manager was Fa'ahivalu Taumoepeau.

I was part of the deck crew, and I was responsible for safely guiding ships in and out of the harbor. When a ship arrived, I wore a rope around my neck, swam out using a buoy, and flashed a light to safely guide the ship to shore and help facilitate the mooring line to be attached securely to the bollard. I did the same thing when a ship departed. I facilitated the release of the mooring line and wore the rope around my neck as I swam out, guiding the boat safely out of the harbor. Although this task was physically draining, I still enjoyed it simply because I gained valuable experiences learning about boats, navigational systems, as well as the harbor's operations. Because I was the only one that went to school from our deck crew, I was often enlisted to help at the post office as a temporary worker to cover when someone was on leave. I loved it as I slowly gained experience in the work field.

In 1959, I made a lateral move from being a deck crew member to the customs department as a boarding officer under the direction of Sione Panuve. While there, they realized that I was smart and quick-witted when managing money and understanding the daily operations. Lipoi Tupou was an entrepreneur businessman who owned a store in Nuku'alofa, and he was also the managing director of the post office. He saw my potential as I often covered for those personnel on leave under his watch.

After I clocked out at 5:00 p.m., I walked over to Lipoi's store and worked part-time. Lipoi was the one that showed me the ins and outs of running a business, and I learned the process of ordering goods from overseas and how to clear them through customs. I often asked Lipoi, "Where is my paycheck?" But he always giggled and gave the same reply every time: "Your pay is the knowledge I have taught you about running a business." Although I would have preferred some monetary compensation, I could not argue with Lipoi because I gained valuable knowledge through his coaching.

As my work experiences began to widen, a breakthrough glimpse of a business model came to me, in an aha moment of clarity. A ferry boat operation between islands. This was it: finally a business idea that aligned with my vision. It entered my thoughts almost in a dreamlike stage. I was filled with excitement and hope of a business idea that had been planted in my mind.

My pay at the time from customs was nineteen sovereign (*sovaleni*) every two weeks. As I looked back, I don't know how anyone survived with such low pay, myself included, but I reasoned that working for the government was privilege enough. I used this opportunity to further my life's goal, and I was like a guinea pig, always the first person willing to try anything new. I could not keep my curiosity at bay as I tried to expand the scope of my knowledge and my understanding of the different operations among these three sectors. I slowly learned how to run and operate a business.

Since I got a steady government job, I started to enjoy myself a little bit as a young man maneuvering through life. I attended dances and began to socialize with my peers and friends. At one of the church dances at Matavaimo'ui located in Kolomotu'a, a neighboring town to Nuku'alofa, I met a beautiful young lady named Lu'isa Mataele. We danced together, and out of impulse, I asked her out, and she said yes.

I anticipated our first date with excitement, but I had nothing to offer as an official way of asking a lady's permission for courtship. All I had was a single packet of cheese, so I took that and gave it to her. Although it was considered a lowly gift, she graciously accepted my heart's sincerity. As we became friends and our courtship continued, I became interested in other young ladies, so I often neglected Lu'isa as I followed my heart's desires.

Little did I know that Lu'isa had been praying and fasting once a week on my behalf, asking the Lord's guidance to find her soulmate. I found out later, Lu'isa felt prompted that I was the right person to marry; however, I started to back off from our relationship and pursued other interests. Lu'isa never wavered in her faith; she continued her daily prayers and weekly fast.

At this time, marriage did not enter my mind because I was too busy trying to make a living and started to enjoy my youth. No matter who I was with, something always tugged at the corner of my heart and led me back to Lu'isa time and time again. I could not loosen this emotional hold, as though it was an outside force beyond my own. This gravitational pull always redirected my path back to Lu'isa, so I started to give our relationship some serious thoughts.

Humble Beginning

As we continued our courtship, we slowly learned about each other's backgrounds and shared comparable stories. As the bond of our friendship grew and we became closer, we both fell deeply in love with each other. I finally mustered up the courage and asked Lu'isa for her hand in marriage, and she accepted my proposal. On March 30, 1960, we got married, and it surely was a day of celebration. Lu'isa was twenty-two and I was twenty-four when we embarked on this journey together and established the Uata Family.

Lu'isa & 'Uliti's Wedding Day
March 30, 1960

Before the ceremony, we went to a little photo studio at Nuku'alofa and took a picture to commemorate our special day. We took one in our wedding attire, Lu'isa in a long white flare dress, and I wore a suit. Then we took another photo in our Tongan attire. Lu'isa wore a *puletaha*, a traditional Tongan outfit, and her *ta'ovala*, a traditional mat covering your waist. I also had a Tongan outfit, a *tupenu* on the bottom with a white shirt and tied with a *ta'ovala* wrapped around my waist.

I had no family that attended our wedding because both Mother and Venisi lived far away from Nuku'alofa where the wedding took place. Lu'isa had many of her family attend our wedding, and we had a *kai pola* (a Tongan feast laid out on a woven coconut branch with many good foods). It was indeed a day of celebration as we exchanged our wedding vows. I thought to myself, I am now starting a family of my own, and I have come to embark on another crossroad in my life.

Lu'isa and I moved around a lot during the first year of our marriage. It was a humble beginning for us as we started our own family and began this new chapter in our lives. First, we were at Kolonga living with Mother and Hiko. We stayed with them for a short while. Later we heard about a wetland area facing *Teufaiva*, our national outdoor stadium located in the suburb of Nuku'alofa, and it was almost like a deserted area. It was called the wetlands (*ano*) because when it rained, most of the area was covered with pools of muddy water, with the exception of some few dry spots. The wetland was owned by Tevita Fetuli, and he was kind enough to allow us to build our first home there.

I remember when Lu'isa and I first arrived and started building, other families were there, and we became neighbors with the Po'uha, Lotaki, and Mahu'inga families. We managed to find a dry spot on high ground in this wetland area, and we built a small little round house (*ki'i fale fotaha*).

Lu'isa and I were both resourceful in building our first home. I got leftover crates from work and used that as lumber, then used cardboard boxes to create the interior walls of our little house. We used the plywood from the crates as flooring. You could see the *kelekele* (ground) through the openings, but we made do with what we had. We felt proud when our building project was completed but, truth be told, our home was more like a little hut than a house. Nonetheless, we were still proud that we called this hut our own.

It was difficult to access our little house during the rainy season because we had no option but to walk through the muddy waters. We had boots that went up to our knees, and we used them to access our makeshift dwelling. When we left the house, we hid our boots on the side of a bush, then Lu'isa would sit on the back of the bicycle while I peddled. This bicycle was from work. The area was swarmed with mosquitos, and when we stood on high ground and looked down to the muddy waters, we could see tilapia swimming around. Such was the harsh reality of our humble beginning.

Time was of the essence as Lu'isa was pregnant with our first child, and we needed to move out of the wetlands before our baby was born. While we lived temporarily in this wetland area, Lu'isa was determined to secure a piece of land for us to build a permanent house in the neighboring suburb of Mailetaha. She was on a mission to get on the landowner's good side.

My wife got up early every morning and made *ti ma* (hot tea) by steeping *moengalo* (fragrant leaves) or *la'i moli* (orange leaves) in boiling water, then added sugar and some milk, and lastly, putting *ma pakupaku* (hard crackers) in the tea to soak and soften. She walked over to Fetuli's house and gave him his *ti ma* as his breakfast. What little money we had at the time, Lu'isa used it to buy sugar, milk, and hard crackers so she could make this breakfast for Fetuli while she and I went without.

Lu'isa's daily effort was not in vain, as Fetuli was moved by her thoughtfulness. He granted us a temporary place to build on dry ground; we did not officially own it yet, but that was sufficient for us. We again built a little round house just like the one we built at the wetlands using leftover materials from the customs department where I worked. We put up a makeshift kitchen outside. It was completed just in time for the arrival of our first child.

On February 9, 1961, our baby boy was born, and we named him Venisi Jr. after my brother. We were both inexperienced in parenthood, and further compounded by the fact that we barely had anything to survive on ourselves, let alone provide for a baby. Lu'isa managed to hand sew a couple of *napikeni* (cloth diapers) for Venisi Jr. using random materials she was able to gather. When one *napikeni* got wet, she would immediately *unuunu* (hand wash) it then hang it out to dry, so it was readily available for the next change. Lu'isa often drank hot water with some natural herbs to help her breasts produce milk for baby Venisi because he was growing and needed more milk.

One of the saddest memories I recalled was the day Lu'isa could not get our son to stop crying. She had him suck on her thumb, but he cried and cried because Lu'isa could not produce any more milk that day. It was so sad for me as a young father as I watched helplessly while my son cried nonstop due to hunger.

While I hid out of sight in shame, Lu'isa took control of the situation. She used a piece of cloth and wrapped baby Venisi around her back, then walked with him to Kolomotu'a and asked one of her family members for help. She returned later with milk, and I witnessed a mother's love for her child. I thanked my wife for her bravery because I could not bring myself to beg for milk, but she did it without hesitation to save our son. Lu'isa, in her loving way, said, "I do what is needed to keep our family afloat, and you just focus on work." I felt so much gratitude for my wife. I have been truly blessed with a great woman.

Not long after we built a dwelling on dry land, we got kicked out of the area, and to this day, I don't remember why. We moved in with Lu'isa's family, Peni and Tu'avava'u, in Kolofo'ou, and from there, we moved in with Grandma Fifita's brother Tava and his family, also in Kolofo'ou. While we lived with them, Mother asked her uncle Tava to cut us a piece of his land, and he said okay, he would look into it.

Peni & Tu'avava'u

Lu'isa was resilient and did not give up hope. She continued to provide daily *ti ma* for Fetuli and her persistence won him over. Fetuli gave us the green light to return to Mailetaha as he finally decided to give us a piece of his land to own. We didn't have any money to compensate Fetuli for his generosity, and it was then that I learned he had a soft spot in his heart for my wife. Fetuli felt cared for by Lu'isa when she served him breakfast every morning with the *ti ma*.

The process for getting the deed recorded was exceedingly long and tedious, but time was ticking away, and we could no longer wait. Lu'isa and I decided that it was time for us to build a bigger house to accommodate our growing family, and we did just that. At this time, we were able to afford to build a brick house.

As we gathered the building materials, our neighbors ridiculed us for our foolish actions. Some neighbors even asked us point-blank, how can you waste your hard-earned money building a brick house when you have not officially been named on the land deed? Lu'isa spoke with confidence, "We are building our home based on faith that the Lord knows the desires of our hearts, and He will provide a way for this to happen."

The mockery continued as they laughed and whispered behind our backs that we were delirious by building a home on "shifty grounds," meaning unowned land. But with faith that we were building our home upon the rock of our Savior, we were unmoved even by reality as we stood tall and firm in our conviction that with God, everything is possible, even miracles.

My wife is a woman of strength—physically, mentally, and emotionally, but she is also a woman of great faith and a spiritual giant. Lu'isa was the glue that held our family together. She made our humble dwelling a home and a haven for our family. As the old saying goes, "A mother's heart is the lifeblood of the family." This was certainly true in our home. I've often wondered, when does this woman sleep? Lu'isa is the last to go to bed and the first to wake up in the morning. All day long, she would cook, clean, and tidy up our home, wash clothes by hand, take care of the children, and do other chores both inside and outside the house.

Lu'isa was creative, smart, and energetic as she made do with whatever we had at the time. We both believed that every blessing flowed from God, so in the morning we said our prayers before we began the day, and at night, we said our prayers before we slept. This ritual daily routine became habit, and our prayers evolved from asking for blessings to expressing gratitude for our blessings.

There were times when I wondered if Lu'isa regretted marrying me, but she never showed any sign of regret, self-pity, or discouragement. My wife is my better half, a pillar of light and hope like a breath of fresh air and just a ray of sunshine. When I returned home from work, she always had a smile on her face, and she made our tiny little house inviting and a happy place for us. We laughed and talked together even on days when we had no food, and she always reminded me not to focus on what we lack but be grateful for what we have. Although we didn't have much, we had each other, and our love was strong enough to endure any hardship.

I can truly say that my wife was and still is the glue that held our family together. Lu'isa worked quietly from the background without complaint. She always chose to remain optimistic in lieu of fear. She focused on what we had instead of what we lacked. She always expressed gratitude on bended knees, and thanked God for the sunshine, for the rain, for our health, for my job, for the roof over our heads, etc. For anything and everything, Lu'isa gave thanks. The words of her prayers were our family's power source, a voice of calmness, peace, and hope.

Chapter 6

Rescued

Deep Wounds Healed by Love

December 1960, a young lady in her teens suddenly appeared at our front door and boldly announced, "My name is Toakase Finau, and I am Sioeli's daughter from Ha'ano."

"That is my uncle!" I exclaimed as Lu'isa and I embraced her with a welcoming hug. "Come in. Come in and make yourself at home." Her face was pale from the salt residue of the sea, her eyes tired from the long boat trip, and her clothes dampened from the ocean mist, but otherwise, she

Toakase Finau

was healthy and vibrant. She continued with her introduction. "I was sent by my father to stay with his sister Melepua for school."

I interrupted in haste, "Why, yes, of course. You just stay put right here with us, young lady, as we are family, so no further explanation is necessary."

We sent a message to Mother in Kolonga as we awaited her arrival. Mother hugged Toa tightly with an affection only an aunt can provide. She held up Toa's face to get a good look at her with such a loving embrace. Mother demanded news about Ha'ano, and she emphasized, "Do not leave out any detail." We talked; we laughed as we enjoyed each other's company. At times, we cried as emotions ran high, and I felt like I had known Toa all my life. Hours flew by and it was time for Mother to leave. She asked Lu'isa and I if Toa could stay with us because it would be closer to school since Kolonga was far away due to lack of transportation.

Although our house was small and more like a little hut, we welcomed Toa to our humble dwelling with open arms. That same day, Lu'isa managed to scrape up some leftover materials and made a curtain to at least separate our sleeping spaces.

Toa, at the age of sixteen, came into our lives when Lu'isa was pregnant with our first child, and she was a godsend. Over time, Toa shared her story with enthusiasm and eagerness as she lovingly told us about her family. "There's eight of us, you know, and the oldest is Mele Vavahe'a, second is Finau Vala, third is me, Seini Toakase, fourth is Saia Siale, fifth is Tevita Masiva (who has passed on), sixth is Talanoa Fukakimuli, seventh is 'Aisake Tava, and eighth is Siokapesi Fifita." As she gave an account of her siblings, she paused with each name and cleared her throat as though she wanted to make sure we heard their names clearly. Toa continued, "Our mother, Melenaite Finau, passed away at age forty on October 14th, 1958, then my father Sioeli remarried in 1959 to Hingano."

There was a long silence, then Toa recounted the painful memory of losing her mother. Tears flowed down like rain on her cheeks as she sobbed, covering her face with her hand. After some time, Toa continued, "I will never forget the day my mother passed away. Saia and I mourned over her body from Pangai to Ha'ano. It was a day of sorrow and broken hearts and has been ingrained in my memory forever."

We felt her silent cry for someone to fill the void of her mother's absence, and we felt her pain. Lu'isa reached over, took Toa into her arms, and hugged her tightly with a motherly love and affection. Lu'isa looked into her eyes and whispered, "Toa, please don't cry. I know I can never replace your mother, but if it is okay with you, I will be your mom, and 'Uliti will be your dad."

Toa wiped the tears off her face, nodded her head, and choked on her emotions as she said, "Thank you, thank you both for accepting me. Losing my mother was an emotional tsunami that drowned my soul; but now I can breathe again. I feel like I belong and have a place I can call home." Lu'isa and I gained a daughter the day Toa came into our home at the age of sixteen before any of our children were born, so we consider her our oldest child.

Toa helped us more than she ever took credit for as she babysat for the children and worked side by side with Lu'isa doing daily chores around our home. After school, she helped us manage our little store located right in front of our home. She was a good accountant and made detailed records of daily expenditures and revenues as well as people who bought on credit. She was sharp and talented with recordkeeping, and she quickly adopted a business mindset.

In 1962, Toa graduated from Queen Salote, an all-female high school. After graduation, she went back to Ha'ano to visit our grandma Fifita, who adopted her. Toa discovered that her siblings had all been dispersed and went their separate ways. Mele got married and moved out; Vala was already in Tongatapu and attended 'Atele High School. Two of her brothers, Saia and Talanoa, went and stayed with Auntie Suli in Pangai (the same home that I resided in when I was a kid).

Toa in 1962--Celebrated Passing Exam

In 1961, after the hurricane that devastated Ha'apai and Vava'u, The Church of Jesus Christ of Latter-Day Saints offered free tuition to Liahona, so Saia relocated to Tongatapu and stayed with their mom's family to attend Liahona. Her youngest brother, Tava, lived with their father's oldest sister, 'Ana Siupeli, in Vava'u, and her baby sister Fifita, who was only one year old at the time, had been adopted by our grandmother. Toa felt hopeless and defeated because her siblings had been scattered and spread out among families.

Upon her return to Tongatapu, Toa brought back one of her younger brothers, Talanoa, who was eleven years old at the time. He attended 'Atele, a boarding school for boys, and Saia attended Liahona. When Saia heard that Toa and Talanoa were living with us, he decided to stop by and visit. Every school break and holiday, the two young boys came and stayed with us.

I was worried about my wife and how she felt about my first cousins moving in with us since we barely managed to survive ourselves. But Lu'isa embraced these children with love and cared for them as if they were her own. Although we did not have much of anything at all, we loved my cousins, especially my wife. These children considered us as their parents, so they addressed us as Mom and Dad.

On December 21st, 1965, Toa married Patimi Folau and she moved out and started her own family. Her youngest sister, Fifita, came in 1969 from Ha'ano and stayed with her as she attended Tonga High School. They visited us daily, and Fifita accepted us as her parents. Even though these children grew up and went their separate ways, the bond that we created was so strong, even to this very day. We considered them our adopted children, and they considered us as mom and dad.

Toa & Patini

The details of our fates being intertwined came naturally because of our family ties. But the bond we created rescued children with deep wounds, who left their environment to escape love that grew cold and affection that dissipated with their mother's passing. They felt lost and abandoned and were simply looking for a place to call home.

Lu'isa and I identified with Toa's story as it unfolded, and our awareness heightened as we became sensitive to both her expressed words and silent outcry to belong. We saw ourselves in her shoes, drawn from similar experiences. Lu'isa was born while her parents were on a church mission, lost her mother at the age of five, and was left in the care of her blind father. I lost my father at age four, and, with no hope in sight, I was given the burden of being the provider for our family. Our past experiences, pains, sorrows, suffering, grief, and tears were the things that instilled compassion into our hearts and enabled us never again to allow a child to grow up lacking affection. This was the building block of our newly formed family.

Although we provided Toa and her siblings with basic human needs such as shelter, food, and clothing, she later revealed the deeper meaning of our relationship. For Toa, it was the feeling of acceptance and love she felt from us, especially from my wife, Lu'isa, as she stepped in and took the place of their dearly departed mother, which healed her wounded heart. "Mom and Dad," Toa said, "Because you rescued me when I felt abandoned and discarded, I used the same healing power of love to rescue the rest of my brothers and sisters."

Sioeli & Melenaite's Children: from right to left: Fifita, Tava, Talanoa, Saia, Toa, Vala & Mele

Toa relayed this moving experience with us as she recounted her memories. It happened in November 1966 as she and Patimi returned from New Zealand after they were sealed in the Hamilton Temple. They traveled by boat via MV *Tofua*, and they docked and stopped by Vava'u on their way back to Tongatapu. As she was standing on the wharf, she felt a hand touching hers, and she looked down; it was a young boy with a dirty face in ragged clothing. She did not think much about it, but then she felt the boy's hand again touching hers. She looked down and upon closer observation, she realized that it was her baby brother, Tava. She had not seen him since he was four years old when he was adopted by Auntie 'Ana Siupeli. He was now twelve years old. "This was amazing, because I thought I would never see Tava again," Toa continued. She bent down and hugged her little brother and did not let go of him. She said a silent prayer of gratitude for this miraculous reunion.

A feast was prepared for them as a welcome greeting by the locals. As they began to be seated, someone tried to take Tava away from her and said he could eat later, but Toa would not let go of his hand. She said, "This is my baby brother, and I will take him with me," so they let her be. She eventually asked permission from Auntie to take Tava with her to Tonga, and her aunt agreed.

As Toa shared her precious memories with great emotion, Lu'isa and I felt her gratitude, and the bigger question emerged, what is the worth of a soul? Such question made us search for meaning, and we extracted deep truth from the Parable of the Lost Sheep, told by Jesus in the Gospel of Luke to illustrate the love and compassion God has for every person.

> And so, the shepherd left the ninety-nine sheep in the fold where they are safe and secure, but He climbs up mountains and went down over valleys searching to find that one lost sheep and when he found it, the shepherd shouted with joy, and then he lifted the lost sheep and placed it on his shoulders. He carried the lost sheep on his back until he returned him home. (Evangelist L. t., luke king james version, 2001)[4]

Fast forward to 1983, my daughter Mele Lavinia gave birth to a healthy, beautiful baby girl on February 27th. She named the baby Melenaite Uata Jr after her younger sister (who was named after Toa's late mother). Lavi was still young, trying to figure out her own path in life. Without a husband to rely on, she did her best to balance her life between school, work, and taking care of a baby by herself. Lavi and the rest of our children were living in our home on Cedar Street in Santa Ana, California.

In the early 1970's, Lu'isa and I decided to take our children to the US to have a better education. I stayed behind in Tonga to run our business while Lu'isa took our two oldest children, Venisi Jr and Mele Lavinia and stayed with her cousins in Hawaii. The struggle was real and we decided that it will be best if we buy a home in the

US. Lu'isa had aunties that lived in Hollywood, California, so we flew there to look for a home.

We drove around the greater Los Angeles area then extended our search into the Orange County area. We found a four bedroom, two baths home that we loved on Cedar Street in Santa Ana, CA and we bought that as our first family home away from home. All our children slowly transition to US in search of an education. Lu'isa stayed with the kids until they were old enough to take care of themselves. In the early 1980's, Lu'isa returned back to Tonga and helped me continue to run and expand our business

In 1984, Lu'isa and I flew from Tonga to the US to visit the children. We saw the kids were doing okay despite their individual challenges. On this trip, we visited 'Alisi, Lu'isa's sister. When we arrived at her home, we saw a baby crawling out onto the sidewalk almost to the edge of the street. Lu'isa picked her up, and it was our oldest grandchild, Melenaite Jr. I remember the expression on her face and her words, "Oh, how incredibly sad. No mother nor father to take care of this little baby girl." We inquired as to who was supposed to watch the baby, and we learned that Lavi left her in the care of her cousin while she went to work.

Naite Si'i 1st Birthday Celebration 1984

Lu'isa and I looked at each other with the baby in her arms, and without either one of us saying a word, we both simultaneously decided to rescue this baby due to safety reasons. We flew back to Tonga with our granddaughter and raised her as our own. We loved her just the same as our biological children as well as our adopted children. We called her Naite Si'i to differentiate her from our daughter, Naite Lahi.

This child was bubbly and lively, and she got into everything. She was tough and strong, and she played rough. The girls were timid around her, so she liked playing with boys more as they were tough enough to take her punches. Every time we got a complaint about how naughty Naite Si'i was, Lu'isa defended her and said, "She is only like that because she is full of energy." Later, as Naite Si'i grew older, Lu'isa and I decided to make her adoption official. We went through the legal process, and once it was done, we took Naite Si'i to the temple and sealed her to us for time and all eternity. She was now officially one of our children.

As Lu'isa and I entered our golden years and reflected on our journey as a couple, one thing became clear to us: we each had a difficult childhood and experienced firsthand the pain of losing a parent. Although we did not know it at the time, the invisible hand of God can now be seen as a pattern in our lives. Our marriage and our family were built upon the foundation of our Savior.

We had our ups and our downs, some turbulence and some peaceful moments, some happy times, and some sad experiences through our sixty-plus years of marriage. But through it all, it was the love of our Savior Jesus Christ that kept us grounded. It was His grace that moved us to compassion. It was His mercy that filled our hearts and overflowed with love. We recognize that the Lord rescued us through his love. And now, we paid it forward by doing the same for our adopted children who came into our lives not by birth but by choice, and their wounds were healed with love.

In the tenth Chapter of Luke, Jesus is asked, what is the most important commandment? He responded that the greatest commandment is, "Thou shalt love the Lord thy God with all thy heart, and with all thy soul, and with all thy strength, and with all thy mind; and thy neighbor as thyself." (evangelist l. t., luke king james version chapter 10, 2001)[5] Jesus was then immediately asked who counts as a neighbor, and he responded with a parable that is an example for everyday life.

> The Good Samaritan is a story of compassion. It is about a traveler who is stripped of clothing, beaten, and left half dead alongside the road. First, a Jewish priest and then a Levite comes by, but both avoid the man. Finally, a Samaritan happens upon the traveler. Although Samaritans and Jews despised each other,

the Samaritan helps the injured man. (evangelist l. t., luke king james version chapter 10, 2001)6

Like the good Samaritan, Jesus is always there to rescue, love, and show mercy to us. We both concluded that if we saw these children as burdens, then we would have missed the opportunity to include them as an extension of our family. The Lord used us to rescue these abandoned souls. Lu'isa and I have received blessings a hundred times over, no, a thousand times over from these children, and the resounding message from all of them is, "Thank you for saving us with your acceptance and love." The depth of the love we felt reflected how God's love rescued us during our darkest hours, and in return, we did the same for others. "For God so loved the world, that he gave his only begotten Son, that whosoever believeth in him should not perish, but have everlasting life." (Evangelist J. t., 2001)[7]

God's love is unconditional, and we have witnessed it firsthand ourselves in each of our upbringings. Now, as adults, we emulate that love that we felt from the Lord because it was through Him and by Him that we were saved. By the grace of His love, which knows no bounds and does not discriminate by the color of our skin or play favoritism by separation of class, etc. The sun shines upon the righteous and the sinner just the same, and the rain falls upon the rich and the poor alike. Because of the purity of His love, the magnitude of His grace, and the depth of His mercy, our hearts were moved to act without any reservation. By divine design, we became instruments in the hands of God for His glorious purpose.

Chapter 7

$19 Legacy

Gratitude Turns What You Have into Enough

As I contemplate and reflect on the eighty-plus years of my life's journey, there have been many peaks and valleys. Peeling back layers and rummaging through the school of hard knocks, a pattern emerged. It was truly in the valleys of my life experiences where I had been enlightened and gained wisdom that illuminated the path I walked.

      Gratitude is seeing the beauty of life. It allows the mind to embrace the now and makes the heart surrender to the fullness of the moment. When we see the world through perception of gratitude, something magical transforms our thought process. Even with sadness and disappointments, you smile. Despite rejection and failure, you accept. When doubt and fear creep up, you shut it down. In the face of mayhem, you restore order, perplexity into coherence. Even an acquaintance can turn into a friend. Gratitude makes sense of our roots by understanding our past, bringing tranquility for today, and creating hope for tomorrow.

As I picked apart memories and categorized them into timelines, my thoughts pulled me in like a cyclone of unwanted recollections to drown out the misery of my experiences. But they must be unraveled to understand how a shift in perception helped me through tough times. The life lessons learned in these valleys conceptualized a much deeper level of enlightenment.

Decoding gratitude from a higher consciousness of thought, a spiritual discernment awakened my soul. Greatness begins with a grateful heart. It is humility at its core. Gratitude is the foundation laid for enlightened perspectives and expands spiritual virtues such as faith, prayer, bravery, contentment, joy, love, and thanksgiving.

To imply that I understood these concepts while in survival mode would be an abstract notion of my illusion. But in retrospect, my experiences were byproducts of every choice I made—good, bad, or indifferent. Once this clarity set in, I embraced my past and all its forms because going down to the valley floor allowed me to appreciate the peak of the mountain. As with everything in life, there is a polarity of opposite forces. Without darkness, one cannot appreciate light. Without pain, one cannot appreciate health; without war, one cannot appreciate peace; without sadness, one cannot appreciate joy, and so on and so forth.

When I think back to the struggles and hardships we endured during this poverty stage of our lives, the resoluteness of the human spirit never ceased to amaze me. We were not only broke but broken in every sense of lack and scarcity, both physically and emotionally, and our circumstances stretched us to the limits. Our little family was growing with the birth of our first child, as Toa came and stayed with us so our family's needs increased. I dreaded that time of the month when I handed over my nineteen-dollar pay to Lu'isa. I knew deep down it was scapegoating to force the responsibility onto my wife to use this meager income to figure out how it would last us until next month's paycheck.

To this day, I still don't know the secret recipe that Lu'isa used to stretch such a puny income to manage our household, but she was the queen of budgeting. My wife was undeterred and driven by her love and sheer determination. As if this was not enough, she never murmured, complained, or showed any remorse or regrets. She never once made any derogatory comment or demeaned me as a provider in any way, shape, or form. The only words out of her mouth were, "'Uliti, thank you for working so hard. Thank you for providing for our family. You are the best." Her positive attitude was infectious, and her gratitude made me feel like I could conquer the world. After work, I went *taumata'u* (fishing) and *fangota* (picking up shellfish) to supplement our family's income.

I still remember how Lu'isa took a twelve-ounce can of *kapapulu* (canned corn beef) and divided it in half. She used half to make a stew for us to eat that day, then placed the other half in a small tin with water to avoid ants, which she later used for our meal the next day. She was meticulous and creative in budgeting our needs as she used the skills she learned as a head cook at Liahona.

During mealtime, only the kids and I ate and not Lu'isa. I remember this one day as we were eating, Toa asked, "Mom, where is your food?"

"You eat up. My food is at the *kulo*." Toa nodded her head, but the truth behind Lu'isa's comment is, there was nothing left in the pot except the *vai haka* (the water that the food was boiled in). After we ate, Lu'isa went outside to the *kulo* and drank the *vai haka* as her food. These are but a few examples that demonstrate Luisa's sacrifice for our family.

The appealing aspect of faith gave us hope, even if it was just a spark. It was more than sufficient to make us believe there was a better tomorrow. There were times that I wavered and complained, but my wife was a warrior of the faith. She often quoted Matthew: "For verily I say unto you, If ye have faith as a grain of mustard seed, ye shall say unto this mountain, Remove hence to yonder place, and it shall remove, and nothing shall be impossible unto you." (matthew t. e., matthew king james version chapter 17, verse 20, 2001)[8]

Then, with a smile on her face, she declared, "These hardships are temporary, but we must remain steadfast in our faith. Then and only then will God perform miracles. So, you see, 'Uliti," she continued, "in all things give thanks to God and express gratitude. Let us be thankful for the nineteen cents in our pocket instead of wishing for the ten dollars we don't have. With gratitude in our hearts, God will deliver and turn what we have into enough."

Things became clear that the missing part of this mystical equation was gratitude. As I adopted this mindset, I began to say thank you for everything. Even in my prayers, many times, I found myself not even asking the Lord for anything except expressing the gratitude. I would say, "Thank you, Lord, for my breath. Thank you that I am alive today. Thank you for my family." The more I adopted this practice, the more I became aware of the shifting tide as I evolved. I would smile for no reason at all. I began to admire nature, even the rooster crowing, the dog barking, the cow mooing, and the birds chirping. Everything became music to my ears.

Our circumstance lacked many physical possessions according to the world's standard, and one may ask how we can be grateful in such a mediocre state. But truly, when gratitude fills up the soul, the dimension of the heart expands to a point where you see beauty all around you. The perception of beauty is subjective depending on one's definition and one's own life experiences. One may consider something beautiful, where another would see it as the opposite. As I embraced this gratitude mindset, one verse of my favorite hymn engulfed the ambience of my spirit:

> When upon life's billows you are tempest-tossed,
> When you are discouraged, thinking all is lost,
> Count your many blessings; name them one by one,
> And it will surprise you what the Lord has done
> (count your blessings, 2022)[9]

As I searched through the scriptures for inspiration and words of wisdom, I found comfort and delight reading in the New Testament in the book of Luke about the account of the ten lepers.

> The Savior, traveling toward Jerusalem, passed through Galilee and Samaria and entered a certain village where He was met on the outskirts by ten lepers who were forced to live away from others because of their condition. They stood afar off and cried, Jesus, Master, have mercy on us. The Savior, full of sympathy and love for them, said, "Go shew yourselves unto the priests," and as they went, they discovered that they were healed. The scriptures tell us, One of them, when he saw that he was healed, turned back, and with a loud voice glorified God, and fell on his face at the Master's feet, giving him thanks: and he was a Samaritan. The Savior responded, Were there not ten cleansed? But where are the nine? There are not found that returned to give glory to God, save this stranger. And he said unto him, Arise, go thy way: thy faith hath made thee whole. (Evangelist L. t., Luke king james version, chapter17, verse15, 2001)[10]

As this story indicated, the lepers were instructed to go to the priest, and as they did, all ten of them were healed. However, only one recognized that it was not the priest that healed him; it was Christ. Because this one leper is the only one who recognized the Savior—as the originator of the miracle—he was made whole. He understands that Christ is the Master Healer. He understands that Christ is the Savior. So, he is made whole, not only of physical leprosy but also of the spiritual ailment that distances us from our Father in heaven.

How often do we do this—credit someone who has blessed us and failed to acknowledge that it was God's power that enabled that person to perform such a blessing? I ask this question because there have been many times when I either forgot or completely failed to recognize the invisible hand of God. But upon close observation, it has been evident throughout my journey, in good times and in bad, in lack and in abundance, miracle after miracle.

The bible clearly tells us in Proverbs, "A wholesome tongue is a tree of life: but perverseness therein is a breach in the spirit." (solomon, 2001)[11] I chose to use my words to uplift others, give praise to God, express thanksgiving daily, and synchronize my energy with the source of all lifeforms. As in the words of Albert Einstein, "There are only two ways to live your life. One is as though nothing is a miracle. The other is as though everything is a miracle." (albert einstein, 2022)[12]

> Gratitude is a divine principle. It is a mark of a noble soul and refined character. The Lord has declared through revelation: "thank the Lord thy God in all things…And in nothing doth man offend God, or against none is his wrath kindled, save those who confess not his hand in all things, and obey not his commandments." (doctrine and covenants 59, 2019)[13]

> Choice blessings await those who live in thanksgiving daily. "He who receiveth all things with thankfulness," the Lord has promised, "shall be made glorious; and the things of this earth shall be added unto him, even a hundred fold, yea, more." (doctrine and covenants 59, 2019)[14]

Gratitude is the ultimate expression of appreciation through receiving. If we withhold releasing this emotion of gratitude until material things show up or events happen, then we are still swimming in the shallow end of the pool of this magnetic field. To dive into the deep and swim in the ocean of abundance of gratitude, express appreciation before the blessing shows up. Feel the joy of receiving and saying thank you before the things you wish for manifest.

As a symbol of our gratitude and an expression of our love for the Lord, let us rededicate our lives in like manner and give gratitude and thanksgiving unto God in all things. As we do so, let us not get so wrapped up in just learning about gratitude but actually living its principle. It is a state of being, and it can be practiced in many forms, including meditation, visualization, verbalization, but most importantly, the highest expression of gratitude is measured by the magnitude of emotions felt in the heart.

Gratitude is a countermeasure to negative emotions, an antidote to stress and worry. It is a neutralizer of bitterness, resentment, greed, and jealousy. It is cherishing, savoring, and appreciating everything; it is not taking things for granted but taking delight in the present moment.

Gratitude is a strong and potent cure. It changes your perspective from scarcity to abundance and allows you to pay attention to the goodness in your life. When this powerful shift takes place in your mind and heart, it transforms your state of being to a level of contentment of elated happiness.

The nineteen-dollars-a-month budget is sixty-three cents a day, which had to feed, house, school, tithe, and obtain the necessities of life for our whole family. The question arose as we see it from a realistic perspective—how? This is easily an impossibility that the mind cannot fathom.

We find yet another example of the invisible hand of God that made the unimaginable possible and taught us that abundance is not what you have, but rather it is a miracle of the Creator and Savior. That even two loaves of bread and five fishes fed a multitude of thousands. (Proverbs king james version, chapter 15, 2001)[15] So, it is not about how we survived such poverty with sixty-three cents a day, but instead, it is about the invisible hand of God that provided for our family with only sixty-three cents a day.

Lu'isa and I both attest to this constant truth that has shown up again and again throughout our journey. We can honestly say with great humility, singing praises of thanksgiving daily to our Savior, that His ever-present love encompasses all humankind, the sweetness of His grace surpasses all understanding, and the reach of His tender mercy defies all logic. His example pointed to the crowning moment of His prayer in the garden of Gethsemane, where every pore of His body bled and He submitted to God's will, "O my

Father, if it is possible, let this cup pass from me: nevertheless, not as I will, but as thou wilt." (evangelist st., 2001)[16]

His ultimate sacrifice is a similitude of His unconditional love as He took on the sins of the world, asking nothing in return. Then, on the cross of Calvary, as recorded in Luke, "And Jesus had cried with a loud voice, he said, Father, into thy hands I commend my spirit: and having said thus, he gave up the ghost." (evangelist l. t., luke king james version chapter 23 verse 46, 2001)[17]

There is one thing I know with certainty—a grateful heart fuels the essence of the soul and sends out a vibrational field of energy that resonates with a higher source of power. The more we feel gratitude, the more abundance and blessings we are attracting to ourselves and the happier we become.

Chapter 8

Unexpected Miracle

Opportunity of a Lifetime

A breakthrough came for our family—a miracle unfolding. One day I was going over the accounting books with Lipoi and I discovered this huge ledger from the customs department. It detailed deposits for every cargo shipment that arrived at the port of Nuku'alofa. They used the deposits to calculate the taxes owed on each cargo freight, and any excess amount left over would be refunded to the depositor once an invoice was received.

The law at the time stated that if excess funds from a deposit were not claimed by the depositor, the funds would be put into a government account and held until an invoice was received before funds were released. Over the course of several years while Liahona was under construction, their planning and development department always made a deposit with every shipment. This was done to allow the building materials to be released immediately so there were no delays to the construction project.

It was now 1963 and the construction project for Liahona had already been completed ten years prior, in 1953. Yet there was a huge amount of money still in the government's account from Liahona, and I could not help but wonder why that was the case. I felt a sense of duty to my alma mater, so I went to Liahona and requested to see their ledger pertaining to the construction. I gathered all the bills of lading and invoices that were submitted to the port authority and put them in chronological order. I then calculated the duty tax for each shipment bill of lading according to the entry in the government ledger and matched them up to Liahona's ledger.

As I went through the records with a fine-tooth comb, I learned that many invoices were never submitted to claim a refund of the excess deposited amount after each shipment. This finding was mind-blowing as I learned of the substantial amount of money still floating in the government's account. I decided on my own that I would return the excess funds to the school that gave me an education. For months I worked tirelessly to identify which deposits had been invoiced and paid and the ones yet to be invoiced as Lipoi continued to allow me access to the ledgers because I was helping him with his monthly reports.

I detailed a report of the outstanding invoices, and I took the information to Liahona and submitted them to Principal Lindsay for review, then I left. I felt good as I used the knowledge I gained to pay it forward to my beloved school. Weeks went by, then I received a request to come to the Liahona administration office. First, I thought that I made a mistake, but Mr. Lindsay came around and hugged me and said, "Brother Uata, I could not believe what I saw on the report you submitted and that it was never detected by the school staff." He continued, "I thank you on behalf of Liahona for the work you did. My audit and bookkeeping team had looked over the report and they all concurred that it is all correct. We have submitted all the unclaimed invoices and the government has refunded all the money owed to the school."

I replied, "It was my absolute pleasure, and I am happy to hear that Liahona got their money back." We chatted for a while and as I said my goodbyes, Mr. Lindsay said, "Wait, Brother Uata. I have something for you as a reward for the work you did."

I pushed his hand away and said, "It is okay, Principal Lindsay. Liahona had given me so much, and what I did was a token of my appreciation."

Lindsay insisted and said, "Then accept this reward as a token of Liahona's appreciation," and he put an envelope in my pocket. I felt conflicted. On my way home, I kept asking myself if I should have taken this reward or not. Part of me said yes but another part of me said I should not have taken it. I decided not to open the envelope until I got home so Lu'isa and I could open it together.

When I reached home that evening, I put the envelope in front of Lu'isa and she gave me this weird look then asked, "What is this?" I began to explain that this was a reward from Liahona and before I finished with my explanation, she ripped the envelope open. We had never seen so much money before. Our jaws dropped open as we feasted our eyes on the money laid out in front of us. Lu'isa teared up as she asked me repeatedly if it was true we could really keep the money.

I reached over to my wife's face and wiped her tears dry. We then looked over at our two little children, still babies, and our hearts swelled with gratitude. We both knelt in humility, and I offered up a sincere prayer of thanksgiving as I returned all glory back to God for this unexpected miracle. As we acknowledged His hand in all things, even the depth of His love defies all logic and comprehension. I was all choked up with emotions as I became speechless. We knelt in silence for some time, then my wife's hands reached out to mine and held it tightly as I finally managed to end our prayer.

Unexpected Miracle

This reward money from Liahona was an unexpected miracle. Unbeknownst to us that such blessing would flow through to our little family, made us both pause and ponder on God's grace. We both agreed that our family comes first, so we decided to use the reward money to go to the temple in New Zealand and seal our family for time and all eternity.

The trip was long, hard, and exhausting, but well worth it. We departed Tongatapu as a group with other families in a boat called the MV *Tofua* to Vava'u. Lu'isa and I and our two babies, Venisi (two years old) and Mele Lavinia (one year old) boarded the MV *Tofua*. From Vava'u we continued the boat journey to 'Apia, Samoa, then to Pago Pago, Samoa. From Tonga to Samoa, the distance is roughly 550 miles. We continued to Niue Island, which is roughly 400 miles from Samoa. From Niue we continued the boat ride to Suva, Fiji, which is roughly 700-plus miles. We then took a bus ride from Suva to Nadi and boy, it was rough and bumpy. From Nadi, Fiji, we flew in a Teal airplane to Auckland, New Zealand, and we were greeted by Peesi Harris. We were taken to an LDS chapel. We then took a final bus ride from Auckland to Hamilton, where the temple stood.

I clearly remember this experience as we finally laid eyes on the temple. We were in awe as we gazed upon this Holy House of the Lord standing majestically erected on sacred ground. An eruption of cheers and hand-clapping roared throughout the bus. We were so moved with emotions that tears filled our eyes and we began to sing songs of praise. Our spirits heightened with gratitude, as we gave thanks to the Lord Almighty for His protection and ensured our safe arrival. After a rough trip of about two weeks' time, we finally beheld this beautiful and glorious sight.

Hamilton, New Zealand Temple

The day we entered the temple, we were astonished with its majestic view. The temple stood tall and grand as the most elegant structure we ever laid eyes on. As we entered through the entry way, there was an atmosphere of stillness, and if you were to speak, it was in a whispered tone to respect and maintain the quiet atmosphere within. Beautiful paintings hung on the walls, and magnificent furniture was found throughout as we walked through its hallways. But the icing on the cake was the moment we knelt on the altar of the temple, and Lu'isa, Venisi Jr., Mele Lavinia, and I were sealed as a family to be together forever, for time and all eternity.

1963 Lu'isa, Uliti, Lavi & Venisi in front of the Hamilton Temple

Nothing could have prepared us for such an experience. The expression of love and peace permeated the room all around us and the feeling of joy and happiness filled our hearts. Such memories so precious and irreplaceable. Lu'isa and I both received confirmation that we made the right decision regarding this miracle that came to us in such an unexpected way, and we felt our prayers were answered.

I expressed to the temple president my desire to receive my patriarchal blessing as I had prepared myself spiritually to hear what my Heavenly Father had in store for me. President John Haubee was both the temple president and the patriarch that gave me my blessing. As he laid his hands upon my head and called me by my name, "Brother 'Uliti Uata...," I felt a surge of energy flow throughout my entire body. In stillness and in reverence, I quieted my mind to fully absorb this spiritual experience. I listened intently to every word uttered by Patriarch Haubee and heard it line upon line and precept upon precept.

The spirit confirmed to me that God knows me individually, and I was so moved by the blessings that the heavens had in store for me. I said silently in my heart, "Thank you, Lord, for Thy love and Thy tender mercy. Thank you, Lord, for this precious gift that I can use as a guide to navigate my way through my earthly journey. I don't know what I've done to deserve such blessings, but I have received them with gratitude."

As the time drew close for our return trip home, I could not help but ponder on the privilege and honor we had to serve in the temple of God. I felt renewed, alive, a sense of purpose, and a connection to divine power beyond my own. When the day finally came for our departure, we sang hymns of praises on the bus and lifted our voices to give thanks. I said an earnest prayer of gratitude silently as we drove away.

    The trip back home was long, difficult, and rough, to say the least, as the ferocious power of the ocean pounded its waves against the boat, but I was so elated with pure joy that it did not faze me one bit. My gaze turned toward my wife and saw her beautiful smile as she rocked our babies to sleep. There was no fear in her facial expression but faith, no doubt but hope, no anxiety but peace, no worry but content, and no uncertainty but firmness. What a blessing to have a woman of strength by my side and feel her calming presence and great love for me and our children. She puts out such positive vibes and she radiates serene energy of light.

    About two weeks after we departed New Zealand, we finally had a visual of our tiny island and we were able to see the coconut trees from a far distance. I thanked the Lord for keeping us safe on our journey. Although Tonga is small—after all, it is only a dot on the world map—it is my home.

    Upon our return, it took a couple of days to recuperate from the long and arduous trip, then it was back to normal life. I continued working for the customs department but, soon after, I received a job offer from Liahona to be a business manager. Another huge blessing, and I took it in a heartbeat. I immediately quit my government post because the pay Liahona offered was $216 every two weeks, which was tenfold what I was making at the customs department and much more than I ever expected.

    I could not believe how blessings flowed into our family and I became keenly aware of God's grace and how He is mindful of our circumstances. There are times that our faith will be tested and there are times we have to wait patiently for answers to our prayers, but I am convinced that when we endure things well, whatever life throws at us, there is a silver lining even in challenging times.

    I felt I had come full circle where I was right back at Liahona, my beloved school. At this time, each department ordered their own supplies, but the principal decided that every order would route through me for review and signing off so the books would be correct and accurate. It was not long before I was promoted to work for the church's mission office in Nuku'alofa, where I was now the business manager for all the church's finances and constructions, which included Liahona High School and all the chapel construction projects.

The jobs from the church along with the gift that I was awarded from Liahona had been an unexpected miracle for our little family, and this was the breakthrough that we needed so badly. Things started to change little by little. Going back to the point I made earlier, the Lord is mindful of our needs and He knows our heart's desires. He knows of our struggle and suffering. He knows of our pain, our heartaches, and every teardrop that has been shed. He is aware of it all, and just as a caterpillar starts to create a cocoon to transform into a butterfly, so too must our earthly journey go through the same process. As the butterfly struggles to push its way through the tiny opening of the cocoon, it pushes the fluid out of its body and into its wings. Without the struggle, the butterfly would never be able to fly.

Symbolic to our lives, it is in the valleys that we grow. It is in the struggle that we become strong and acknowledge that there is a higher power other than ourselves. And as Albert Einstein said so eloquently, "There are only two ways to live your life. One is as though nothing is a miracle. The other is as though everything is a miracle." (einstein, 2022)[18] I choose the latter, for when I look back on my life, it has been nothing but miracles. To say that I was grateful would not adequately depict the depth of my feelings.

The story of David's anointing as king as told in the bible speaks of a deep spiritual truth. When the prophet Samuel questioned the Lord, the answer came, "But the LORD said unto Samuel, Look not on his countenance, or on the height of his stature; because I have refused him: for the LORD seeth not as man seeth; for man looketh on the outward appearance, but the LORD looketh on the heart." (Samuel, 2001)[19]

Unexpected Miracle

If anyone were to ask me back then what I did to have such miracles manifest in my life, I would have simply answered, I do not know. But now that I have reached an old age, with more understanding through years of experiences, I will boldly say that the Lord looked favorably upon my family because of the gratitude both my wife and I have always demonstrated regardless of our circumstances. For we embraced it all, the good, the bad, and everything in between, and have always returned all glory back to God. For we are weak and He is mighty; we are finite and He is infinite; we are dust and He is eternity. We are nothing without God. The words of the prayer of Saint Francis of Assisi speak the emotions I feel deeply in my soul:

> Lord make Me an instrument of Your peace
> Where there is hatred let me sow love.
> Where there is injury, pardon.
> Where there is doubt, faith.
> Where there is despair, hope.
> Where there is darkness, light.
> Where there is sadness, joy.
> O Divine master grant that I may
> Not so much seek to be consoled as to console
> To be understood, as to understand.
> To be loved. as to love.
> For it's in giving that we receive
> And it's in pardoning that we are pardoned.
> And it's in dying that we are born...
> To eternal life.
> Amen. (A prayer of St. Francis of Assisi, 2021)[20]

Chapter 9

Year of the Dragon

Business Launched

Nineteen sixty-four was the Year of the Dragon in the Chinese Zodiac, and things slowly began to shift for my family for the better. We received yet another special gift from God as this was the year my third child was born. A beautiful daughter, precious in her own ways. She was perfect.

In our Tongan tradition, naming a child is important because the person a child is named after has a story and is chosen for a reason. The "namesake" carries the name with honor and pride. My first cousin Toa had been with us for a couple of years and had been an angel sent to our family and helped us raise our children. We asked Toa to do us the honor of naming the baby and without hesitation she named her "Melenaite" after her late mother.

I felt the blessings flow out from the heavens and rain upon our family. Never once did my wife and I ever take anything for granted. We were profoundly grateful for everything we had, and in everything, we gave thanks. I started a small store right in front of our home at Mailetaha and it was doing quite well. I started to assess my current situation and knew that I must do more, but what?

I already stretched myself thin every day doing odd jobs here and there on the side in addition to my main job at the Tonga Mission, just to bring in extra money to support our growing family. But the nagging feeling I felt years earlier returned, except this time, with urgency. To be a provider, I cannot be an employee. I must run a business and be my own boss. I must step up and do more, for I have not exhausted all avenues of my potential and my gift bestowed to me by the Lord.

I went back often and read and reread my patriarchal blessing so I could fully comprehend it all. And the thing that stood out in my mind were the words that I am from the tribe of Ephraim, who was said to be greater than his older brother. I later learned that when Joseph brought his two sons to Jacob to be blessed, Jacob crossed his hands and gave Ephraim the blessing of the older and to Manasseh the blessing of the younger.

> And when Joseph saw that his father laid his right hand upon the head of Ephraim, it displeased him: and he held up his father's hand, to remove it from Ephraim's head unto Manasseh's head. And Joseph said unto his father, Not so, my father: for this is the firstborn; put thy right hand upon his head. And his father refused, and said, I know it, my son, I know it: he also shall become a people, and he also shall be great: but truly his younger brother shall be greater than he, and his seed shall become a multitude of nations. (moses, 2001)[21]

I found similarity between this story and within my own family. My brother, Venisi, is older and I am younger, yet I have been bestowed the responsibility of being the provider. Armed with this knowledge, I began to dream to provide not only for my immediate family but for my extended family as well as for my Ha'ano community.

I started to envision myself as a businessperson. I dreamed of a day that I would not have to worry about financial matters. I dreamed of helping my brother run his own business and building a home for my mother where she could rest from her labors and just enjoy life. I dreamed of helping the people of my hometown of Ha'ano and the people of Ha'apai have access to transportation via the ocean. However, I did not speak of these dreams to anyone as I might have been labeled a man with a wild imagination for my circumstance at the time dictated otherwise.

Although fear and doubt stood out in my mind as a blockage to my dream, I also asked the question, what are the alternatives? If worse comes to worst, I will fail as a businessman, but better that I try and fail than giving up before I even gave my dream a chance. As I did this self-talk in my head every night before I slept, I began to envision my dream in my own virtual reality and the question remained unanswered—what are the alternatives?

In the morning I began my day with a prayer seeking earnestly the Lord's help. I thought to myself, if God brought our family out of poverty from the lowliest of places, then God will certainly see us through anything. So, I mustered up the courage to look fear in the face and take a leap of faith anyway. Boy, did it pay off.

I became an entrepreneur literally overnight, even when I didn't fully understand the concept. I kept my job at the Tonga Mission as my primary source of income, but I used the skills I learned from Lipoi Tupou on my business venture. I approached Lipoi to allow me to piggyback on his shipments from New Zealand and he said yes. Excited to see his student thrive, Lipoi helped me through the process. Once Lipoi's order was in place, I included my own order for a whole leg of lamb called a *carcass* and I bought it for like four pennies per kilo.

At this time in Tonga, it cost twenty cents per kilo for lamb, so I figured this would be my starting point. Once the shipment arrived, because of no refrigeration, I had to sell it the same day. I threw the leg of lamb over my shoulder then hauled it on my bike to smaller stores. I sold it to them for wholesale price and I made profit this way. This was hard labor and exhausting work but oh so worth it. With my first shipment being a success, I made a second order, then a third and so on until I was able to obtain my own shipment. I began to dream bigger as I envisioned a store in downtown Nuku'alofa.

It wasn't long before my dream came to fruition as my entrepreneurship skills and hard work paid off. I was able to secure a storefront in the heart of downtown Nuku'alofa at Penitome's home and that was a success on its own. Then I thought, if this is possible, what else is possible? My dream became bigger and bigger and so did my vision for the future. Things began to change almost instantaneously overnight for my family as opportunities began to come out of nowhere and doors opened everywhere.

In the same year, I had saved up enough money from what was left over from our temple trip to New Zealand along with some profit we made from the store and I was able to buy one car. Instead of using it for our family needs, I decided to start a taxi service also located in downtown Nuku'alofa at the home of Maka Siteli, and it was known as the Red and White Cap.

Our family still walked everywhere back and forth between our home in Mailetaha and downtown Nuku'alofa to help run our store business and this small taxi service I started. Soon after, the profit received from this one car increased to two cars and I bought one after another. The business started to take off and the *Tu'ipelehake* (the King's brother) honored us by bestowing a name to my family's taxi service, *Leimapa 'o Mailefihi,* and his son, Prince Mailefihi, came and

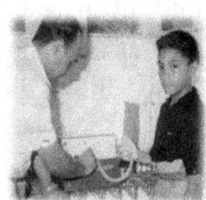
Prince Mailefihi Officially Opened the First Taxi Services

officially opened our taxi service. Soon the taxi service outgrew its current location so it was moved to the Fatafehi Road (*Hala Fatafehi*). I handed the taxi business over to Venisi and told him to run this business so he could make a living for his own family. My brother took over the taxi business and he renamed it the Tonga Holiday Taxi.

The successful business ventures did not stop there. I managed to obtain a second storefront, again at the home of Maka Siteli, and not long after that, I established my third store in Nuku'alofa at the home of Moala Bella. In the meantime, I explored the transportation services. I bought a bus that serviced the route from Nuku'alofa to the west side (*Hahake*). This was a great success as it provided a more affordable mode of public transportation for our people. Just when I thought that my hands were full, I felt another nudge to try the tourism sector.

Business Sign Tonga Holiday Tours & Travel Services

This was a huge market as tourism became popular. I established a beachfront property, a resort at Monotapu, and named the business Tonga Holiday Tours and Travel Services. I added another property on a remote island called Makaha'a as a day resort for guests touring the island. Along with the tour services, I also created a travel agency to assist the locals with their overseas travel arrangements.

If I were to sum up 1964, I would say that it certainly lived up to its name as the Year of the Dragon as all these businesses emerged as if they sprouted from one source. The three stores in Nuku'alofa, the taxi service, the bus transportation, the tour guide business, and travel agency all began and were established in that year. I could not attribute their success to my own doing because I acknowledge the hands of the Almighty performing miracle after miracle every step of the way as I took a leap of faith with every business venture I started.

Now that I had established a lifeline for our family to survive on, it was time to move on to bigger dreams to include the people from my hometown of Ha'ano. With this goal in mind, I was on to my next business venture of ferry boats and shipping services. My vision of obtaining a boat became more and more real to my mind and I knew it was just a matter of time.

In 1965, I decided to quit my job at the LDS mission so I could fully dedicate my time to running a ferry boat and shipping business. In the meantime, Lu'isa and Toa took over the operation of the stores and other businesses I had started. The mission president at the time was John H. Groberg and his Tongan name was known as *Kolipoki*. The mission had a boat named *Faifekau* (Missionary) and the church wanted to sell the boat for liability reasons. Many people were interested in buying the boat, but President Groberg, knowing my desire to run a boat business, gave me the opportunity and I bought the boat. This was the first boat I ever owned; it was my pride and joy and I proudly renamed the boat *Pulupaki,* which is the name of a shore in my hometown of Ha'ano.

*John H Groberg--
Mission President*

The whole concept of a boat floating on the water carrying passengers and freight from one island to another had captured my imagination for a long time. I was so intrigued with its concept that I decided to dive in and fully invested in this line of business. I began to embark on the idea of building a boat, but at this early stage and due to my inexperience and lack of resources, I had to focus on my next move.

I started a business of an inter-island ferry with my first boat, MV *Pulupaki,* and it was a venture of the unexplored. I decided to start with a simple route between Tongatapu and 'Eua since the distance between the two islands is only twenty-five miles. I wanted to test how the business via waterways would turn out and it proved to be profitable and a huge market, especially since it is the main source of transportation between islands in Tonga.

1st Boat-Purchased--Faifekau later renamed as MV Pulupaki

I started with one service run of the *Pulupaki* from Tongatapu to 'Eua and each voyage was filled to capacity with ferrying not just people, but agriculture as well. People from 'Eua transported agriculture to Tongatapu to be sold at the marketplace, and it was a big advantage that allowed the locals to easily exchange goods and services. I was absolutely blown away by the huge waves of opportunities that the open sea offered. The MV *Pulupaki* was not big enough to offer services to Ha'apai and Vava'u, so I kept exploring new ideas of how to expand this service and build an infrastructure that could accommodate a larger fleet of inter-island ferries.

'Uliti Uata, Pres White, Tonga Toutai in 1968

It was an exciting time in my business adventures as everything seemed to have exploded into full bloom in just a couple of short years. I was more energetic than ever to ride the waves of its success. I felt a sense of accomplishment at this rate of growth and how the businesses advanced to new heights as it expanded rapidly. However, there was no time to relax as I became laser-focused on the inter-island ferry business. Just when I thought I had a full plate of commitments, the very first stake of The Church of Jesus Christ of Latter-Day Saints was established in Tonga in 1968 and it was called *Stake Nuku'alofa Tonga*. President White was the stake president, first counselor was Tonga Toutai, and I was called to be the second counselor.

I was humbled by this calling as I considered myself unworthy of this honor; nonetheless, I could not decline as I do not understand all things. The Lord has called me to be of service to help build up His kingdom here on earth, so I willingly obliged and accepted this calling. I drew strength as I reflected back to the story of King David's anointment.

Even though I did not know how to fulfill this calling, the Lord trusted me with it, so who am I to question His anointed? The Lord qualifies whom he calls. I went through a phase of self-assessment because I could not help but wonder if I was ready for such a huge undertaking as with this calling came great responsibility. Although my answer was clearly no, I am not ready to serve in this capacity, but I also took a leap of faith as I kept repeating to myself the Lord's words to Samuel: "Men looketh on the outward appearance" and may judge me for my imperfections, "but the Lord looketh on the heart" and found me worthy in His sight.

    This became my truth and I accepted my calling with reverence and humility. Once this belief sank in, I no longer judged my imperfections, my unworthiness, or my shortcomings as a man. I only focused on serving in the capacity I had been called as I saw myself as only an instrument in the hands of God

Chapter 10

Lighthouse of Hope

Story of the MV *Ongo Ha'angana*

Broadening the scope of my businesses and increased services for the inter-island ferry route dominated my thoughts after I bought my first boat, the MV *Pulupaki*, in 1965. I began a habit of waking up at five a.m. and started my day with a run, then by six a.m., I put all my children in the car and we drove to the Faua Wharf. Once there, the kids occupied themselves in the car while I stepped out and stood right at the edge of the wharf and turned my gaze outward, looking toward the horizon.

Lighthouse of Hope

I have always felt the ocean calling me, so I answered the call by being present daily at the waterfront. I began to dream as I listened to the sounds of the waves, imagining a boat that could handle such a mighty and turbulent yet vast and magnificent force. This dream was my lighthouse of hope.

I did not understand my own actions at the time as to why I would do such a thing, but looking back through the lenses of time, I became keenly aware of why I religiously took my children to the wharf every morning even though I could not explain it to them. I wanted my children to enter my imaginary world so I could share with them the unfathomable energy I felt from the sea.

This almost senseless routine became the battleground between my conscious and subconscious mind. My faith and my belief told me that there was much more out there for me to accomplish. It was both therapeutic and almost hypnotic as I explored the unknown in my mind and allowed my imagination to just run wild. I have respected the sea since I was a young boy for its deep and treacherous nature. Once I conquered the outrageous ideas in my mind, I was able to subdue my doubt and my fear and I rose to the occasion and brought forth my dreams so that they could materialize.

When I was little, looking out into the ocean was an escape from reality as I allowed myself to contemplate and ponder a better future. The sound of its waves summoned my lingering thoughts to break free and allowed my imagination to flow and took me on an adventure around the world. To some people, books immerse them into the story, but for me, just breathing in the ocean breeze and hearing the waves allows me to flee the reality of the moment. Now that I am older, my memories of the past keep me captivated by the waters, almost like a euphoric state of being.

All my business ventures were born out of my imagination while I looked out into the ocean, because it was the pathway that connected me to my past. The memory of my four-year-old self is like a lingering shadow. The image, the sound, the smell, and the feeling, are all carried within this one memory. The ocean was my exit from reality and the entryway to my creativity. As I buried my thoughts in the sounds of the waves, I emerged to undisclosed possibilities.

My lighthouse of hope was nine years in the making as I built layers upon layers of finding a way to have it manifest into a reality. The major hurdle was finance, so I began saving and I lived a very frugal life. I was very meticulous in bookkeeping and made sure to account for every expense and income for my business. The money I made from the MV *Pulupaki* generated a lot of revenue and all the profit I made from my first boat had been saved to invest in my dream of expanding the inter-island ferry. I thought of taking out a loan, but it quickly subsided when I considered how much interest I would have to pay, so that idea got thrown out quickly and the only option left was to pay cash. So, I hunkered down and stuck to my plan.

One side was the finance and on the other was the planning process. I envisioned my goal and I started working. There were times when I felt discouraged and wanted to give up the ferry boat service idea because I already had many other businesses to take care of, but that meant giving up on my dream. And because I have always had the attitude that failure is not an option, I knew that I was left with no choice but to keep going and keep pushing myself. Year after year I re-evaluated my goal and made notes of the progress as well as any setbacks that I had encountered.

When I shared with Lu'isa the burden I felt, she would rub her hands over my head and say, "This head belongs to the smartest man I know, and 'Uliti, you can do anything once you commit your mind to it." I always laughed and asked her why she had so much confidence in me, and her reply was always the same: "Because I have seen your capabilities and I know that you do not allow anything or anyone to stand in the way of your dream." She continued, "I know you have an iron will, and if the first option does not work, you explore a backup plan." These are the kind of encouragements my wife always gave me. She would hype me up with her words and it rubbed off on me. Whenever discouragement started to sneak up, her words lifted me up and pushed me to find a solution to whatever it was that I was facing.

After nine long years of mulling over my dream, I finally had enough cash on hand to transform my vision into a reality. In 1974, I decided to build a boat large enough in size to accommodate servicing Ha'apai and Vava'u. The pathway to my lighthouse of hope started to take shape and my excitement could not be contained. My quest started and soon the plan rolled out and the architecture and the design process began. The boat was seventy-four feet in length and it was the largest boat ever built on our island. The construction was done right next to the Faua Wharf. The head of this construction project was Paula Hemaloto, a huge undertaking for a local builder, but I had confidence in his ability.

We worked almost nonstop except on Sundays. The idea for the construction was that the boat would be built on a slipper so that upon completion, it could be released and the boat would roll down on the slipper right into the waters. The boat was built with the toil and sweat of local workers without the help of modern technology. Nonetheless, it was a project of sheer determination and willpower. There were many setbacks, but nothing really fazed me for I had gone through many worse things in the past. When I heard someone reporting a problem, my answer was always the same, let us find a solution. I reverted to what Lu'isa always said, if that option does not work, figure out a backup plan. Her words of encouragement became an anchor for me to use as my lifeline support. My prayers became more fervent and my faith became firmer and stronger.

After two long years, the boat was finally completed in 1976. It was a day of celebration, a victory for the local builders. This was one of those moments in life when your joy takes you to a whole new level of gratitude. We decided on the day to release the boat to the waters and I woke up early that morning and went to the wharf with excitement. We were all there with workers fired up with a sense of accomplishment to see their labor materialize. The ropes that anchored the boat to the slipper were finally cut loose as we anxiously watched for the boat to roll down to the waters. But the boat did not move.

Someone quickly suggested we obtain the government's forklifts to help the boat roll down the slipper and we all agreed it was a good idea. The forklifts were dispatched, they all arrived, and from all angles the forklifts tried to jerk the boat off to roll, but the boat would not budge. All day we kept trying and trying to figure out what went wrong with the launching process. By now the sun was starting to set and sadness swept over me as I anticipated the worst-case scenario.

The king of Tonga, King Taufa'ahau Tupou IV, commissioned that I come to the palace for consultations. Upon arrival, I gave proper greetings, then we conversed as he inquired on the status of the boat. After he listened to my report he said, "'Uliti, I suggest you do not try anything before it causes damage to the boat. I will have someone contact Fiji for help tomorrow." I expressed my gratitude for his help then slowly made my exit. As I drove back home, I kept thinking of all the possible outcomes, then realized that at this point, I had nothing left except to rely on my faith. When I got home, I was too exhausted to even talk so I immediately went to bed.

I could not sleep as I tossed and turned in bed and kept asking myself, why is this happening? Have I not planned things out properly?

At the crack of dawn the next morning, I knew in my heart that I must ask in faith. I woke up and called all my children to the room for a family prayer. Lu'isa was sick and could not get up. I reached over and held her hand and assured her everything would be okay. I said to my family, "Today I ask for all your faith combined with mine so that we may inquire for the Lord's help." I began our prayer and my voice cracked due to my deep emotions. After some time, I composed myself and cleared my throat as I fought back tears then continued to offer up a prayer from the depth of my soul.

I don't remember the exact phrases I used, but the content of my prayer was as follows: "Dear Heavenly Father, on bended knees we bow our heads and lift up our spirit to request help from Thee. I have done all that is humanly possible to do as I labored on this boat for two years, and now my work is done but not completed. Will thou reach down with Thy Almighty hands and finish the work I have started? For I know that when we reach the end of our efforts, that is when You begin. For what is impossible to men is simple to Thee, and what is inconceivable and unattainable to men is easy to Thee. Thy will be done, and I shall accept it without complaint as I surrender it all unto Thee."

After this reverent prayer, I said to my family, "It is all in God's hands now." I left and drove out to the wharf and I stood there gazing out into the ocean as I prepared myself to accept God's will. After a while, the thought came to me to ask for the forklift one more time. I called to dispatch the forklifts and I was told that all were currently in use except for one, so I asked for that forklift to be delivered to our worksite. I arrived to find the workers standing around the boat with downcast eyes and I could feel their anxiety and their worries. I immediately started to cheer them up, but it was difficult to remain optimistic when the odds were not in our favor. Many workers spoke of defeat, but I refused to allow that negative energy to enter my mind. The forklift finally arrived, and they all wanted to know what I was planning to do. I told them, "Honestly, I don't really know, but I felt a prompting to ask for it again and I did, so here it is." The forklift went into position and with just one jerk, the boat rolled right down into the waters.

Ongo Ha'angana Launched Day—Uliti and the Construction Workers

There was an eruption of cheers, hoorays, hallelujahs, and thank you. As everyone was hugging each other, giving high-fives, fist-pumping, and celebrating this huge victory, I knew it was a miracle from the heavens. I quietly slipped away to a corner so that I could return all glory back to God as I offered up a humble prayer of gratitude for His invisible hand rescuing my work. The only words I felt worthy of expressing were, "Thank you, Lord, for completing the work I could not finish."

The King of Tonga, King Taufa'ahau Tupou IV, honored us with his presence at the opening ceremony (*hopoki vaka*) *pea ne fakahuafa 'ehe Tama Tu'i 'ae vaka koe MV Ongo Ha'angana* (and he named the boat MV *Ongo Ha'angana*). The origin of this name came about because of the reputation of Nobel Malupo of 'Uiha and Nobel Tu'i Ha'angana of Ha'ano. Legend has it their ancestors were unrivaled heroes and warriors with unsurpassed intelligence as well as unmatched spiritual faith. So, whenever the nobles of these two islands ('Uiha and Ha'ano) got together, they collaborated and synergized their strengths and resources, outperforming all of the Ha'apai Group in any given area; hence the name, Ongo Ha'angana.

As the boat went out to sea for the first time, it took me back in my memory to when I stood on the sandy beach of Ha'ano the day my father passed away, aimless, and hopeless. Today, I looked out into the open sea with hope and determination as the horizon looked brighter. The MV *Ongo Ha'angana* serviced both Ha'apai and Vava'u just as I had envisioned, and I was ecstatic to see how much this inter-island ferry service helped our people with their transportation needs. The revenue generated by the boat was more than I had anticipated, but, more than the economic benefit, it was the satisfaction of a mission accomplished, a dream come true. It was such an invigorating and priceless feeling, a sense of honor and duty, yet humbled by the lives that had been blessed by this service.

Only two short years into MV *Ongo Ha'angana* being in service, while on one of its trips in 1978, it capsized, keeling over coral reefs near 'Utungake, Vava'u. When I received the mayday call over the radio, my first question was, "Any casualties? Over." "Negative, over." "Anyone overboard? Over." Negative, over." "Anyone hurt? Over." "Negative, over." My knees buckled and I found myself on the floor. "'Uliti come in, over. 'Uliti come in, over." By the third call, "'Uliti come in, over," I finally came to my senses.

I breathed a sigh of relief and said a silent thank-you prayer for the lives saved, then I began the operation for a rescue mission. This night was long and exhausting; every ounce of energy had been drained out of me. The dawn was breaking and once I confirmed all passengers and crew had been rescued off the boat, I broke down and sobbed like a baby. Part of me cried as an expression of my gratitude to God for the lives saved and part of me cried grieving for my boat.

Venisi and Sione Kalekale took a crew to assess the boat to see if it could still be saved. They reported back that it was possible; however, my brother told me bluntly that it would be both costly and time-consuming. My answer was firm and unwavering, "Do whatever it takes to bring back the *Ongo Ha'angana*." The painstaking righting technique to reverse the capsized boat took months, but when the boat was able to float, it was hauled back to Tongatapu and deliberately docked at Tukutonga awaiting repair.

A song was composed to commemorate the MV *Ongo Ha'angana*, and in it, I expressed my deep feelings for this boat: "Kuo to 'i moana si'ete konga koula, ka he'ikai tuku ai 'eku fie fai fatongia, ki hoku kainga moe Pule'anga Tonga." *"My precious gold was lost at sea, but it does not deter me from wanting to serve my people and the government of Tonga."*

Although the damages were severe, I still wanted to salvage my boat. Our crew worked to repair the damages and it took an exceptionally long time, not to mention the expenses, but the effort was well worth it for me. I emerged from this defeat stronger than ever and the MV *Ongo Ha'angana* was able to resume its ferry service, and Tevita Tai was named the new captain to continue with the boat's operation. I was grateful that I was able to save my lighthouse of hope.

Chapter 11

Conquered Crossroads

Early Years in Parliament and Business Progression

My path had met many crossroads; some sadness and joy, some failures and successes, some hardships and achievements, some regrets and victories, some fear and yet leaps of faith. But all and all, my life has been both tumultuous and exciting, but never dull. I experienced many close calls and heart-wrenching moments, but I also received countless blessings and have witnessed many miracles that cannot be explained. As Mother's words so bluntly stated, it is what it is, and I couldn't agree more.

My passion and my vision were of my utmost desire to be of service to the people of Ha'apai. Whether by inter-island ferry boat service or other means, if I could contribute somehow to make things easier for them, I would do so without hesitation. This wish fulfilled allowed my imagination to explore new interests, even when it was outside the scope of my expertise. Whatever crossroads my path will intersect, they are already conquered in my thoughts. Whatever new heights my journey will take, they are already acquired. Whatever paradigm shift my mind will conceive, it has already adapted.

I began dreaming about my next business venture, and I wanted a central location in Nuku'alofa for all my stores. I started inquiring about a multi-level building and looked into the scope of what this project would entail. I began searching for an architect to draft a blueprint and give an estimate of how much it would cost. For three years I was consumed with this idea, and I was relentless in exploring options for a centralized location for all my businesses. I didn't share my idea with a lot of people except for my wife and my family because it might seem too far-fetched, but I remained optimistic and kept chipping away thinking about this building project.

At the same time, my persistent desire to serve the people entranced my curiosity about politics as I wondered how much more help I could be for the people of Ha'apai if I became their voice inside the government. This crusade fortified my aspiration and soon, I found myself campaigning to be a parliamentary representative from the district of Ha'apai in the election of 1975. I went back to my hometown after leaving its sandy beaches when I was just a boy, flooding my memories with flashbacks. Even the emotions were surreal as I felt the sadness and the emptiness of saying goodbye and recalling Mother's white handkerchief waving from a distance until it faded out of sight.

My first stop was to my hometown of Ha'ano, the main island within the four adjacent islands of the Kauvai Ha'ano Group, which are Muitoa, Ha'ano, Pukotala, and Fakakai. I was astonished as time seemed to have stood still and ceased to exist because everything appeared the same, just as I remembered when I was young. The only obvious change was how the islands were quickly losing their population as people migrated to Tongatapu to educate their children and in search of a better life. Our reunion was caressed with tears of joy due to our deep connection and I felt loved. The people of Ha'ano embraced my return as though a lost son had finally come home. The void of my absence left a hole in my heart that was constantly yearning, longing for affection, and now it was filled up with warm hugs and intimate cuddles from the people I consider family.

    I attended many kava gatherings as men huddled around and sat in a circle telling stories of our ancestors and the proud heritage of my tiny island. I did not do much talking; rather I listened to how legend had been passed on from generation to generation simply by storytelling, and I was engulfed by this beautiful way of preserving history. The men sang tunes of folk songs (*hiva faikava*) with someone playing the guitar and ukulele, and everyone in the kava circle harmonized to its melody as I closed my eyes, reminiscing on the words of each composer telling a story with words that painted a vivid picture of heartbreaks, separations, yearnings, memories, history, and triumphs. Each song invoked a message of the perseverance and courage of human nature, of acceptance and endurance, and ended in a hopeful tone. I was mesmerized by this beautiful artform as it transcends and permeates the soul as only music can reach such depths. I became present at that very moment. Ah, what a transformative experience. This kind of intimate social gathering left a deep impression that makes the heart hunger for more, and I felt honored to be in such company.

    My next stop was 'Uiha, which is my grandfather Saia's place of birth. The people of 'Uiha welcomed me with open arms, and I felt accepted and right at home. I learned more about my grandfather's side of the family and what a rich history they have. It was exhilarating as I heard narratives of different events in history, and I was intrigued by the stories being shared. I came to understand the close-knit relationship between these two islands of my roots. I felt a sense of belonging, a sense of pride, and a sense of patriotism.

As I went around to different islands in the Ha'apai Group, I shared my vision of representing them to the government and

Venisi Uata

having their voices heard. Campaigning was a new concept for me, and I had no manager nor any direct affiliation with experts in this area. My entourage was some of my closest friends who rallied by my side for support and cheered me on, but I had to do the heavy lifting on my own. I knew early on that my campaign message would only resonate in the hearts of the people of Ha'apai through the extent of my sincerity.

How do I appeal to the public's interest? How do I convey the message that I genuinely wanted to be a servant leader for Ha'apai? To that end, I did not campaign on concepts that were far-fetched and unattainable. I did not speak of some abstract idealistic viewpoint. I did not give false hope nor speculate on some hypothesis theory, and I certainly did not make any promises I could not deliver. The message I communicated to the people of Ha'apai was simple and direct: "Allow me to be your representative to the government so that your voices may be heard."

My biggest supporter was my brother, Venisi. He was my number-one fan, and he spoke of my vision as though it was his own.

Uliti's 1st Term in Parliament & His Colleagues

He campaigned on my behalf passionately and he took my cause and made it his own. With my brother's support, I took the message of my conviction to the people of Ha'apai. Every island I campaigned on, I delivered the same message: "If you elect me, I will speak on your behalf. I will fight so that your voices can be heard." I charged forward affirming my belief as I declared with confidence that I was the best person for the job.

Nineteen seventy-five was an historic year as Tonga celebrated its one-hundred-year anniversary since the constitution was established by King George Tupou I in 1875. This was also the same year that I was first elected to parliament, and I felt a huge responsibility on my shoulders as I began to commence my political career. I was ready to take charge of this new crossroad and I entered with the thought, I have already succeeded. I worked tirelessly and made sure the voices of the Ha'apai people were heard in parliament and I delivered on my campaign promise. I was ecstatic serving in this new role and I came to love the law as I also found a new hidden talent that I did not know I had. Standing tall and speaking up as I charged forward to deliver the needs of the people of Ha'apai became my newfound passion.

While serving in parliament, I continued to grow my business. After three years of contemplating the quest to build a building right in the heart of Nuku'alofa, I decided to go ahead with my plan. I secured a plot on the corner of Uelingtoni Road and Taufa'ahau Road. After many years of this planning process, we were ready to rock and roll.

Lu'isa & 'Uliti at the 1975 Parliament Opening

Nineteen-seventy-six, at age forty, I completed my boat project, and that was a huge undertaking that I was proud to have successfully launched. But I didn't stop there, because I was now a year into my building project and I felt a renewed surge of energy in both my newfound passion for politics as well as my business. I felt fearless as I ventured off with different business ideas, which I conquered and succeeded at at every crossroad I encountered. The project was a five-story brick building, and head of construction was Sione Toutai. And just like I did with my boat project, I did not take out any loan as I had saved up enough money to pay cash for the building project as well.

Months after the devastating news of the MV *Ongo Ha'angana* in 1978, the building project was completed and it was a healing mechanism for me as I channeled my energy and focus on the building instead of dwelling on the loss of my boat.

The building erected and stood tall and glorious as the King of Tonga, King Taufa'ahau Tupou IV, commenced the opening ceremony and named it the 'Uliti Uata Building. Among honored guests were the royal family, noblemen, government officials, public figures, local authorities, church leaders, business acquaintances, family elders, neighbors, and friends. It was a proud moment in history as I humbly acknowledged that this was the tallest building ever built on our island. The ceremony commencement was held on the rooftop of the fifth floor and the view was beautiful.

Uata Building Opening Ceremony 1978

Relatives close and extended, friends, and especially the people from Ha'apai made food and laid it out in a *pola* (feast) style in Tonga. Music was playing and amplified by loudspeakers, and the echo of the music traveled and reached all corners of the capital. *Tau'olunga* numbers (a traditional Tongan dance) as well as other Tongan numbers were performed and people jumped up and danced along to the beat of the music. This type of invigorating bliss is called *mafana,* when you feel a warmth inside that makes you instinctively jump up off your feet because the music moves you and releases an emotional state of joy that cannot be contained. The atmosphere was festive and exuberant, hopping and riveting. It was indeed a celebration of a lifetime.

I closed all the three stores I had and moved them into the building as a central location that occupied the ground floor as both a supermarket and a hardware store. On one side of the ground floor, Luisa occupied that space and operated the Pacific View Restaurant, which was growing in popularity and drew in customers for her famous meat pie. I used about seventy-five percent of the second floor and opened a movie theater called The Super Star, and the rest of the floor was used for our

Melenaite Sr, Lu'isa & Siumalu on the Opening Day of the Uata Building

office operations. The remaining floors (three through five) were utilized as rental office spaces.

My business was booming, but my focus was more on the responsibility of representing the people of Ha'apai. Inside the political arena, there was a clash between the nobles and the people's representatives. I totally disagreed with this system of governance because I believe in a democratic society where the will of the people rules. I knew what I wanted but felt powerless to push the agenda. I served two terms in parliament for a total of six years, and I fought vigorously on my campaign promise to represent the voice of the people. However, it felt like fighting a losing battle due to the overarching framework of a constitutional monarchy system.

I did not get into government during the 1981 election, so I figured this was a good time to break away from politics and just focus my energy on building my business. However, the passion I felt about the political system was still burning inside of me like a flame that refused to die out. I decided to build my political muscle and prepare myself to re-enter politics. In the meantime, I focused on the economy and how I could help the people by providing jobs as I expanded my business. I felt liberated when I hired workers knowing that their salary would help put food on their families' table. As I remembered how poor my family was when we grew up, I wanted to alleviate that burden of the families that I employed.

I realized I enjoyed being a businessman and it was not just to make money and profit. It was more for the joy I felt as I gave back to the community. I used my business to provide local employment and serve others from the overflow of blessings that I have been given. I believe that to whom much is given, much is expected.

During this time, I felt like I was doing okay, but the memory of my past haunted me and I couldn't help but feel empathy for families who struggled. Now food was easily accessible for my family, but there was a time that we went without. When I looked at our table full of food, I wondered how many unknown numbers of families probably had nothing or little to eat.

When these thoughts came to mind, I could not help but feel compassion. When I said our prayer, I expressed gratitude for the boundless blessing upon my family and at the same time, asked for blessings upon those who are in need. I asked the Lord to help me magnify my gift so that I may use it to serve others.

Chapter 12

Pivotal Moment

Liahona Alumni Association

Nineteen seventy-eight was a roller-coaster year and a burst of adventure; it was unbelievable and unforgettable. On one side it was full of anguish and sadness, and to the polar opposite was triumph and glory, and I was on both sides of the spectrum. I experienced a devastating blow when the MV *Ongo Ha'angana* capsized, and I was sad but hopeful. The same year, when the 'Uliti Uata Building was completed, I felt an exhilarating sense of joy yet still unfulfilled.

    I could not dissect my emotions. I could not comprehend my feelings and I needed to find a balance to these two extremes. But what could it be? How could I lay to rest my sadness of grieving the loss of a ship that was built by sweat and tears, then shift gears to such a high and blissful accomplishment but still felt empty? It felt like an unsolvable puzzle trying to close the gap between hopeful and unfulfilled and find an arch that connected them so I could have some balance.

I found that when I was occupied with my business and attended parliament sessions, my day was filled with endless things to be taken care of, until I was exhausted in the evening. Only to wake up the next morning and begin the same routine all over again. My spirit started to be weighed down by the mundane daily responsibilities. I justified in my mind that I had too many things to take care of and I was tired because I overextended myself. Just when I started to believe this thought, something pulled on the string of my heart and I could no longer ignore it.

I started to pray more fervently and more intentionally as I searched for answers to this riddle that had plagued my thoughts. The words of the scriptures stood out in my mind: "Inasmuch as ye have done it unto one of the least of these my brethren, ye have done it unto me." (matthew t. e., matthew king james version chapter25 verse40, 2001)[22] But what exactly does that mean? My mind became clear, and I distinctively knew the answer was service, but what does service mean? What exactly does it look like? And in what ways can I increase my service to the people of Ha'apai and my community?

My mind was racing trying to figure out what kind of service I could provide to help in the community, because I thought I was already providing a service to Ha'apai by being their representative in Parliament. My thoughts always took me back to my younger years and how tough it was for Mother to provide for our little family. But the most demanding thing was trying to raise the money to pay for my school tuition. I thought, I am in a position to help families who are in the same situation as I was. I wanted to give back to the school that gave me the education and got me to where I am today.

A year earlier, in 1977, I started a conversation about creating an alumni association for my alma mater, Liahona High

School, but it was only a hopeful thought. This concept got me excited again, and I began to see it as my calling for service. I wanted to get other people to buy into this idea because I knew this task was a huge undertaking and I needed people to see my vision. I sought out old school friends and talked to them to see if they were willing to help recruit other members.

We often held meetings to brainstorm how best to approach this task. I explained to them my vision of starting the Liahona Alumni Association and how it could benefit the community as a whole. As I spoke passionately of how the scholarships would benefit students who were fatherless or motherless, orphans, or from poor families alike, I choked up with emotions and the room became deadly silent. Then someone stood up and clapped his hands, breaking up the awkward quietness, and then the room erupted with cheers. I continued as I expressed my sincere desire to free families and students from worrying about educational expenses, let alone putting food on the table.

I found joy as I discussed this concept among friends, a purposeful goal. Then, like a lightbulb, came a moment of clarity. I finally found the answer of the missing piece to my puzzled mind. I felt fulfilled as I saw this as an opportunity to be able to provide service on a larger scale. Now that I found the answer, I began to have more questions. How do I go about it? How do I bring my vision to life? How do I sell this idea so others can join forces to make this dream a reality? I was so enthusiastic about my vision that I spoke of it to whomever I talked to. Even if our discussion was on a different subject, I often steered the conversation back to the alumni association and how wonderful it would be to help, even if it was just one child at a time.

Few of my good friends bought into my vision. Tonga Toutai, Vaha'i Tonga, Sione Tu'alau Latu, and I started campaigning to establish the alumni association. In 1978, the Liahona Alumni Association officially started. Many of our alumni colleagues joined and we had a huge turnout, more than we imagined. Their contributions were far and wide as each person brought to the table their own unique strengths, which boosted our campaign strategy. Here are a few of the names that I remember:

> Tonga Toutai, Vaha'i Tonga, Sione Tu'alau Latu, Viliami Sika, Sione Sika, Pita Vamani, Semisi Kioa, Nanasi Fine Sekona, Vili Harris, Solomone Toki, Tu'iasoa, Vili Pasi, Vuki Tangitau, Molonai 'Ita'ehau, Heneli Vea, Niua Latu, Moa Tunu, Maile Finau, 'Afa 'Ulufonua, Hoa Fonua, 'Ana Fonua, Paula Muti, Sisi Muti, Tangikina Malu, Selai Latu, Talau Fine, Halahuni Langi, 'Ana Langi, President Uasila'a, Meleane Uasila'a, Teuila Uasila'a, Tali Uasila'a, Kalo Mataele, Kauasi Mataele, Toti Mataele, Toakase Folau, Venisi Uata (SR), and Lu'isa Mataele Uata.

These people that I have mentioned are a short list of the thousands of Tongans who have contributed so much of their time, money, and energy to build up the Liahona Alumni Association. So, if I have failed to mention your name on this very short list, blame it on old age. But, without a doubt, the alumni association was built through the blood, sweat, and tears of so many dedicated men and women, who believed in this worthwhile cause. Having said that, I thank each and every one of you sincerely for your help and donations as we helped, one child at a time.

During our first open meeting, they nominated and elected me to become the first president of this organization. As I delivered my acceptance speech, I felt emotional and almost speechless. I remember saying that I was deeply honored but can't remember much after that. Another thing that I remember, whether it was only in my mind or I actually verbalized it, is that I saw my position not just as the president to lead this organization but as a call for action to serve our community.

During my first year of being the president of the Liahona Alumni Association, I had to attend a weekly meeting with the principal of Liahona to identify the needs of the students. In one of my many trips to the Liahona campus, as I entered the principal's

Uata/I Don't Remember My Father's Face

'Uliti Uata--First Pres of The Liahona Alumni Association, Speaking at First Meeting

office, I was told to wait as he would be out shortly. While sitting there, I heard him scold a student for being constantly late. Afterward he came out and apologized for the delay and started to tell me about the student. He said, "I have put this student on probation and told him that if he is late again, he will be expelled." I then inquired about the reason and the principal said, "I do not know the reason. I just know he has been constantly late every day and no matter the punishment or consequence, he just cannot make it to school on time."

I politely said to the principal, "With all due respect, Sir, did you even inquire as to the reason for him being constantly late for school?" and he said, "No, because this student refused to explain. He willingly accepted his punishments and did not give any explanation."

Soon other members came in and our meeting started. My attention was with this young student, but I could not let the issue go and the principal sensed it. After the meeting, the principal asked me to stay behind, and he called the student back into his office. Then he said, "'Uliti, you have a point, and I too am curious to know what reasons the student will give for his repeated tardiness. I will leave you with this student and trust that you will find the answer." A knock came and the student entered. The principal excused himself out of the room and left us alone in his office.

At first, I just wanted to put this young man at ease, so I began by making small talk and asked about how he was doing, his hobbies, and his schooling, but no answer came. I continued, "You can tell me about your family. How many siblings do you have?" Again, no answer came as he dropped his head downward and made no eye contact with me. I continued, "I am sorry if I have offended you somehow. I just wanted to know a little bit more about you and your situation. I know you have a valid reason for being late, but I don't know what that is so I can help you. I promise you will not get in trouble."

This young man slowly raised his head as his eyes reached mine with tears streaming down his face as he uttered his response, "Both my parents have passed away and it is only my little sister and I left to fend for ourselves. So, in the morning, I get my little sister dressed and take her to school, then I run all the way here, but no matter how fast I run, I am still late." I felt my heart pounding faster and faster by the second. I tried to control my emotions as I felt this young student's pain because I identified myself in his story, as the feelings had not escaped me when I experienced the loss of my father. I felt chills down my spine for that moment as I relived my own personal loss. A memory buried so deep in my subconscious mind that when it surfaced, the feeling was still raw like it just happened yesterday.

This experience confirmed to me the purpose of the Liahona Alumni Association, and this young man's story was the fuel that ignited the passion I felt deep in my soul. I became committed and passionate for this cause, my burning desire to rid poor families of financial worries about their children's education and help support orphans and the fatherless or motherless children to have an education for a better future.

I traveled thousands of miles, even outside the borders of our tiny island to build the alumni association with this mission in mind. I flew to New Zealand, Australia, and the US, going from city to city, calling on the Tongan people that had gone to Liahona High School to help with this cause. My children were grownups but not mature yet and some had just started a family of their own and most of them were living in the US at the time in our family home on Broadway Street in Santa Ana, California.

I remember this experience from one of my many trips campaigning to secure funds for the alumni. We had dinner and one of my sons, Tu'i, said, "Dad, how can you ask us to donate to the Liahona Alumni when we can barely support our own families, let alone feed them?" His question was harsh to hear, yet his point was well taken, and, in that moment, I could not bring myself to give him a politically correct answer to his question. I felt his doubt in this cause I was pursuing and I began to question the effectiveness of my campaign if my own children did not believe in my vision.

There was awkward silence, then Tu'i attempted to cut the intensity of the moment by saying, "Well I am full, and I thank you, Mom, for the lovely dinner," then he emptied his half-eaten plate into the trash can. Moments later, I found myself walking over to the trash can and picked up my son's leftover chicken thigh that he didn't quite finish, and I held up the piece of half-eaten chicken and said this to my son as well as the rest of my children that were present, "To you, this piece of half-eaten chicken is trash, but to the poor, it is gold because your trash can feed them so they don't go hungry."

The intensity of the moment grew as my children all sat up with eyes wide open and their faces had this look of wonder, and I continued, "You see, kids, I am not asking you to take away from the food on your family's table, nor am I asking for you to sacrifice their needs. All I am asking is for you to eat the food on your plentiful table and if there are any crumbs that fall off to the floor, share that with the Liahona Alumni Association, because even crumbs can help to educate poor children." What had happened that day was a miracle on its own as I finally found an avenue for my voice to express my passion.

I took this message everywhere I went. First, I told the story of the young student at Liahona, then I ended with the message I taught my children. The organization grew faster than we had ever expected during the first three years of my presidency. I was elected again for a second term, and I continued being the president. Each year we would have an annual event of the alumni and a certain city would host the gathering. It would normally be like a four-day event from Thursday through Sunday, and this was when we would get the most donations. The hosting began in Tonga, then went overseas to Auckland, Hawaii, Los Angeles, San Francisco, Salt Lake City, and Australia, and the rotation of hosting cities continues to this day.

It was a fun time. Great memories were made as we gathered and socialized with many festivities, and the Liahona Alumni Association grew like a tight-knit community. It was also a time of prideful display of great talents including musicians and composers of traditional Tongan numbers such as the *lakalaka* and *ma'ulu'ulu*. And to top off the event, it's the performance of the Tongan *tau'olunga,* where a young lady performs a solo dance with graceful movements, her hands telling the story of the song to which she is performing. Many cities competed for bragging rights as to who fundraised the most donations. This annual event motivated people to travel from afar to attend and it was fun, yet helped fund the alumni to provide more scholarships for students in need.

By the end of my sixth year of service, someone else was elected to be the president, and I was thrilled knowing that the association was strong and thriving. As years went by, the donations started to dwindle and I felt saddened by this, but I also could not continue to hover over the operations, so I let it go. For three years, the alumni almost plateaued and it felt like the momentum had ceased to exist, but I refused to accept that because the vision I had of the alumni was still burned deep in my heart. When the next voting time came, I was reelected to be the president. This time, I wanted to give it my all during this three-year term.

On the day I was elected president, I made an announcement during the annual meeting that I would increase the alumni's donations to reach one million dollars in revenue. This amount was unheard of, especially on our tiny island. Maybe in America or other rich countries where a million dollars is a drop in the bucket, but to Tongans, no one even heard of this insane amount, and I was ridiculed for this high goal I set. Many deemed it a failure before it even started. Most of my closest friends that I thought believed in me even had their doubts and told me, "'Uliti, you are a dreamer," and I answered unapologetically, "Yes, I am."

I immediately got to work and I flew out to every city I visited before and called for meetings to rekindle the hearts of the people with the association's vision. I went back to the story of the young man that was constantly late and ended with a plea like I told my children, "I'm not asking to take away from your family's needs. You go ahead and eat with your family and enjoy your meals, but if there are any crumbs that fall off from your plentiful table, please share that with the alumni. Because even crumbs can fill up a hungry child's belly and educate a poor child's mind."

This message resonated with people's hearts, and they started to reach deep down into their pockets and share what they could, and the donations poured in left and right. I felt like I had started a movement of bringing to light the struggles of poor families in Tonga. I humanized their struggles and put faces on the issue. Everywhere we went, we witnessed miracles of what moved the heart at its core, the human connection. I shined the light on the needs of those who are less fortunate.

I did not take credit for this success, because no one has power over human emotions. All I could do was share stories of experiences that resonate with people in a sincere and humble way. And by doing so, I did not appeal to their logic, but I appealed to their hearts. By the end of that one year, the alumni raised more than two million dollars in donations, which far exceeded and doubled what our original goal was.

I felt proud as a leader of the Liahona Alumni Association. I was able to inspire people, and they took the association's cause and made it their own. This is how we were able to accomplish this unreachable goal. It was one crumb at a time, one donation at a time that added all together to fill the bucket and it overflowed. The alumni were able to issue scholarship after scholarship, which benefited thousands of students.

The far-reaching effect of the alumni cannot be measured by monetary value because it touched so many lives. Not only for those children that received help for their education but also for those who donated. For the giver felt fulfilled knowing that they had an influence in a child's life. The alumni gatherings brought communities together and gave people a sense of purpose. They donated and shared what they had, not because they were forced to give, but because they were moved to give, and they freely gave.

Serving as the president of the Liahona Alumni Association was a pivotal time in my journey. It has enriched my life as I came to feel the overwhelming joy of giving through acts of service. I came to understand the words in the bible that God loves a cheerful giver: "Every man according as he purposeth in his heart, so let him give; not grudgingly, or of necessity: for God loveth a cheerful giver." (2 Corinthians king james version, 2001)[23] Through acts of service, both the giver and the receiver are blessed as one gives freely and the other receives gratefully.

Chapter 13

Ocean of Dreams

Ferry Boats and Their History

No matter how much I tried to distance myself from my painful past, I could not loosen the grip of its hold. It was almost like a gravitational force beyond my own, circling and tossing around my emotions like a powerful tsunami with no regards to anything in its path. The memory that kept resurfacing was the echo of my mother's anguished cry at the beach that fateful night. Deny it or bury it; it cannot be ignored.

    Why do I always feel a special connection to the sea? What is so magical about the waters? Upon close examination of this unwanted recollection, the mystery pieces began to fit like a puzzle taking shape. The ocean was my escape. My innate ability to drown out the noise of the world and align my energy with nature was my bridge to a parallel universe.

I remembered the calmness that infiltrated my soul by the sound of the waves through the evening tide. I remember the gentle breeze of the wind blowing on my face. I remember staring at the vastness of the deep blue water as I imagined sea creatures living and thriving at the bottom of the ocean floor. I remember wondering what lies beyond the endless horizon as far as the eye can see. I remember how the visuals of these memories were my enchanted forest. And from that space, I was able to disengage from the harsh reality of life.

This pattern of conscious escape to my illusional universe was my safe haven of retreat. Even as a child, I began to harness this dream space and fine-tuned its parameters to evolve in time. Dreaming was an escape from reality. The ocean was my pathway to allow my imagination to run wild and took me to places of wonderment and exploration of the great unknown. I continued this regimen religiously as a young man and even as a father. Every morning, I took my children to the Faua Wharf as my favorite pastime activity and stood in awe before the great ocean and began to dream of a fleet of boats floating on the sea's surface.

In the islands, the only way to alleviate people's transportation needs was to utilize the sea as a connecting point to other islands or the sky via aircraft. Ferries were and still are an essential mode of transportation in Tonga, a sprawling island nation, and elsewhere in the Pacific. I had many business ventures at the time, and, from the outside looking in, one may say that I took on too many responsibilities. But from the inside looking out, I saw endless possibilities. These thoughts were the fuel that ignited my curiosity and that pushed me to be comfortable being uncomfortable.

My querying mind piqued as I became more vigilant to find options for the transportation needs of Ha'apai. I explored not only a route via the ocean but also via the sky. I decided to take bold actions, so I took a leap of faith into an unfamiliar business venture.

'Uliti & his Business Partner Mr. Wayne Fowler

In 1977 while I was still working on the building project and the *Ongo Ha'angana* was still under construction, I partnered with Mr. Wayne Fowler from Olympia, Washington in the US and started an inter-island airline service. I owned fifty-one percent of the business and Mr. Fowler owned forty-nine percent. King Taufa'ahau Tupou IV named the airline Tonga Air Services and he was the one who officiated at the opening ceremony at the Fua'amotu Airport.

King Taufa'ahau Tupou IV Official Opened the Tonga Air Services

This new business venture felt like a shot of adrenalin rushing through my body with much anticipation and excitement. I dared the road less traveled in spite of the risk factor. I was thrilled with the fact that I had broken new ground as the first Tongan to own an airline business. My contribution to our island was acknowledged by Tonga Liuaki, author of the book *Taufa'ahau, Tu'i Ha'apai*. In an excerpt from his book, Mr. Liuaki placed me as number fourteen on the list of prominent individuals who contributed to the growth of Tonga:

"'Uliti Uata. Fokotu'u 'ae 'uluaki kautaha vakapuna mavahe 'a ha Tonga. 'Uluaki fale fungavaka fai'anga pisinisi. 'Uluaki vaka fefolau'aki uta koniteina fakalotofonua 'a ha Tonga. Kautaha taxi mo e falekoloa lahi." (Liuaki)[24]

Liuaki's book cover

Translating the above quote to English:

"'Uliti Uata. First Tongan to have an airline business. First Tongan to construct a multi-story building for businesses. First Tongan to have an inter-island ferry-boat service for passengers and cargo. First Tongan to have a taxi business and big chain stores."

Liuaki's book first page

I expected support from the Tongan government as a local businessman and requested exclusive rights to service the outer islands of Tonga. But, to my surprise, it was denied. I soon learned that I faced fierce competition from SPIA (South Pacific Islands Airways), an inter-island airline service from Samoa, as the government refused my proposal.

Three years into the airline business, and I had yet to turn a profit; yet I continued to pour more and more money into it. The operational costs were mounting as I hired pilots from the US to operate the aircraft, along with fuel surcharge, maintenance cost, wages, and overhead expenses. I felt the financial burden heavy upon my shoulders and I buckled under its weight. I resorted to borrowing from my other business operations to help keep the airline afloat, but I was on the verge of bankruptcy. I fell into a deep depression considering the worst outcome. But such is life; sometimes you win and sometimes you lose.

I talked this issue over with Lu'isa and she knew exactly how I felt, but she did not comfort me in my bitterness. Instead, she helped me see the silver lining. She said, "'Uliti, life is a great unknown because we do not know what tomorrow will bring. However, when we feel we have been beaten down, accept it, learn from it, then move on. But you cannot continue to dwell on it. See it as an opportunity, not as a failure, but as an obstacle to overcome." Lu'isa had a way of pulling me out of my dark corners and allowed me to enter the light and assess the situation with clarity and optimistic perspective. Considering the alternatives, I sold the airline to the Tongan government, which they gladly purchased.

As I emerged from the aftershock of my beloved *Ongo Ha'angana* capsizing in 1978, I was forever a changed man. The close call of lives almost lost at sea became a debilitating fear. Although I took a hard hit financially, I knew that I could always replenish the money, but lives can never be replaced. This thought should have been common sense, but it took this incident to bring it to light. I could not articulate my thoughts, but the lingering feelings of doubt washed over me. I knew that I could either see this loss as a defeat or an opportunity to be seized. It was a choice, but we must bear the consequences of our decisions. I can either hide and live under the shadow of my fear or acknowledge my emotions and say,

I'll do it anyway. I chose the latter because it was the only way to move forward.

It was time for me to rethink my business strategy. I knew without a doubt that I needed to return to the core of my passion and my business strength. The first boat I bought was from the LDS Mission and it was originally named the *Faifekau* but I renamed the boat MV *Pulupaki*. The second was a wooden boat I built and it was named the MV *Ongo Ha'angana* and it was the first and biggest boat ever built in Tonga by a Tongan. I decided to expand the inter-island ferry business, so I took the proceeds from the sale of Tonga Air Services and I took out a loan from the bank, which went against my personal belief, but it was a necessary business decision.

In 1988, I flew to Japan with a crew looking to buy a boat from overseas. Our Japanese business counterpart wanted to take us on a tour to Hiroshima. It was important to them that we understand a bit of their history. There was a feeling of reverence when we entered Hiroshima as we learned that this was the place where the Americans used nuclear weapons and detonated the first atomic bomb. We saw the river that many people ran toward to take refuge from the burning inferno. It was estimated that the death toll reached around 200,000 people, and we saw a monument with words that vowed to seek the abolition of nuclear weapons and everlasting world peace. This tour humbled me as I stood and witnessed the perseverance of the human spirit.

'Uliti in Japan Negotiating Boat Deal

'Uliti Signed Contract of Boat Purchase

I broke ground again as the first Tongan from the private sector to buy a boat from overseas. We brought back from Japan a metal boat, and the Honorable Tuita Toluafe, Minister of Land, was the guest of honor in the christening ceremony. He bestowed the named MV *Fokololo 'oe Hau*. And President Eric B. Shumway

Pres Shumway--Dedication of MV Fokololo 'oe Hau

(President of the Tonga Mission) offered the dedicational prayer. The air was fresh and calm with a sense of peace echoed in the tone of his voice. There was sincerity in his deliverance and the humility in his words felt by all that were in attendance that day. A couple of days after this opening celebration, the boat began its operations to Ha'apai, Vava'u, and the Niua's.

In 1989, I built another boat in Tonga but this time not a wooden boat like the first one I built (the *Ongo Ha'angana*), but a metal boat built to the side of Queen Salote Wharf. I hired a Fijian engineer named Manasa to head its construction and the project took two years. In 1991 it was completed and the boat was named MV *Pulupaki #2* and began operations between Tongatapu and 'Eua. After the completion of this project, I purchased a fishing boat named the *Pakeina* and I changed its name to MV *Paki Moe To'i*. I used that boat as a cargo vessel to transport goods to Ha'apai and Vava'u.

'Uliti & Manasa building Pulupaki #2 in Tonga

Completion of Building Pulupaki #2

MV Pulupaki #2

In this same year, I also flew back to Japan with a crew for a second purchase. This time we went to Nagasaki, the city where Americans detonated the second atomic bomb three days after Hiroshima. We witnessed the devastating effect in the area that was flattened by the bomb, after which Japan accepted defeat and eventually surrendered. General MacArthur was the representative from America who signed the treaty along with a representative of the Emperor of Japan,

Prince Fatafehi Tu'ipelehake with his daughter & 'Uliti

and other world allies who ended World War II. King Taufa'ahau Tupou IV named the boat *Volokaile* after a German yacht that capsized in 'O'ua, Ha'apai. I, however, asked His Majesty to grant a name that was related to my homeland of Ha'ano, and His Majesty granted his approval and changed the name of the boat to MV *Loto Ha'angana*.

In 1995 I bought my third boat from Japan, and Prince Fatafehi Tu'ipelehake honored us at the christening ceremony and bestowed the name MV *Tautahi*.

In 1996, one of my boats, MV *Fokololo 'oe Hau*, was on a voyage back to Tongatapu from Pangai, Ha'apai when a storm of high waves tore through the side of the boat, and it was a miracle that the boat stayed afloat. Despite the severe damage caused by waves, the boat

MV *Tautahi*

managed to make it to Tongatapu before it sank. I sent the MV *Puhipaki #2* for the rescue mission to save the passengers and the cargo. Although I was devastated at the loss of my boat, I was more grateful that no lives were lost at sea.

In 1998, I traveled to the US with a crew and bought an aluminum boat for which my son Tevita Tu'i Uata negotiated the

MV *Ikale*

deal. This purchase took place in Morgan City, Louisiana and it was just the body (structure) of the ship and nothing else. Later my son Edward Kay Uata led the crew to put in all the components of the ship to operate, and it was a huge project. Upon completion, the ship set sail by way through the Panama Canal and Tahiti

before arriving in Tonga. The captain was Sione Kalekale and the engineer and head representative for the company was Edward.

The boat arrived in Tonga and because it was purchased from the US, I wanted to name it *'Ikale* meaning eagle, so I had them paint the name on the boat. The day before the christening ceremony, it was customary to approach the guest of honor and ask to bestow a name, and in this case, it was His Majesty King

Taufa'ahau Tupou IV. I went to the palace and did the formal approach, and the king bestowed the name *Ngongo*, which is a type of bird in Tonga but really has no significant features that would stand out. I was not happy with this name so I asked the king to name the boat *'Ikale*, but the King responded, "That's an American name," to which I replied, it should be, because the boat came from America. However, the King had the last word, so I left the palace feeling sad.

Edward & the Ikale Crew

I called the queen, Queen Halaevalu Mata'aho, when I got home and explained to her how upset I was with the name and the

'Queen Halaevalue Mata'aho & 'Uliti

queen said it would be okay because she would be coming with the king tomorrow to the ceremony. I ordered the workers to take a white piece of fabric and write the name *Ngongo* on it and cover up the name *'Ikale*. The queen gave the speech on behalf of the king and at the end she said, "...and so the name of the new boat will be MV *'Ikale*. All in attendance clapped and cheered because everyone knew the story behind the name, and so they pulled off the white cloth and the name 'Ikale appeared already painted on the boat. The MV *'Ikale* mainly serviced between Tongatapu and 'Eua.

In 2001, I bought another boat from Japan and this was the biggest boat in my fleet and the most modern of all my vessels. His

MV Pulupaki #3

Majesty King Taufa'ahau Tupou IV named the boat MV *Pulupaki #3*, and this boat was the most popular among passengers because it was fast and beautiful and it serviced Ha'apai, Vava'u, and the Niua's. The ferry boat business soared with every boat added. We were able to serve the people of the outer islands of Tonga, which was a huge blessing to access ease of transportation through the waterways. It was a mutual benefit of service to both the provider and the receiver, a win-win situation.

In 2006, I bought another boat from Japan. It was a fishing boat. In 2011, I bought the old MV *Olovaha* from the government of Tonga to see if it could be

Another picture of the MV Pulupaki #3

restored, but the boat was too old and after surveys to see what needed to be done, I deemed it not seaworthy, so I took this purchase as a loss and moved on. I sent my son Edward Kay Uata with a crew to Japan to buy a tanker boat to be used as an oil vessel for transportation. The Department of Marine gave Edward the authority to survey the boat and made sure it was seaworthy.

They left Japan and came through the port of Fiji before they came into Tonga, and it was named MV *Punalei*. This boat transported oil, gasoline, and diesel fuel between Fiji and Ha'apai. This service enabled Ha'apai to have easy access to fuel all the time. This was a tremendous help for the people of Ha'apai as it kept their gasoline supply in constant flow. With this service of the MV *Punalei*, I started a gasoline service in Ha'apai

MV Punalei

and I handed it over to my son Edward to run and operate. The last boat I bought was called MV *Atu*.

As I look back at the boats I had built and bought over the years, they were my ocean of dreams. Each one of my vessels was unique with its own purpose and service, and each one with lots of history. Recalling them by name:

1. MV Pulupaki #1
2. MV Ongo Ha'angana
3. MV Pakimoeto'i
4. MV Fokololo 'oe Hau
5. MV Loto Ha'angana

6. MV 'Ikale
7. MV Pulupaki #2
8. MV Tautahi
9. MV Pulupaki #3
10. MV Punalei
11. MV Atu

Of all the businesses I had done, nothing was more fulfilling than the boat operations because it served a dual purpose. I was able to provide a much-needed service and brought my vision to fruition. My dream came true on so many levels, but the most satisfying feeling of all was witnessing for myself the lives I had touched and helped through this business. My commitment and sincere desire to help the people of Ha'apai was my driving force. It allowed me to follow through and keep pushing myself to reach new heights and break new grounds. Running the inter-island ferry boat operations was truly when I felt most alive.

Chapter 14

S. O. S.

Rescue Mission of the MV *Takuo*

May 13, 1994, started out as just another ordinary day but later proved to be anything but. I learned of the passing of Rev. Selu Mafi, President of the Church of Tonga (*Siasi Tonga Hou'eiki*). Many reverends *(faifekau)* from their congregation went around looking for a boat to escort his body back to his hometown of Nomuka, Ha'apai for his burial, but to no avail. Rev. Finau Katoanga, a close relative of mine from Ha'ano, came to me as a last resort. He approached me and appealed to our close ties on our Ha'ano side of

S.O.S.

the family. When he asked for help using our hometown as a refuge for his request, I was moved with compassion.

This was not a decision I took lightly as this would be a special voyage for the MV *Lotoha'angana*, especially considering the financial cost and the last-minute preparation. This request became personal very quickly as I was taken back in time and relived my own painful experience. From Mother's perspective, poverty robbed us of providing a proper burial for Father, a memory that shook me to the core. Feelings of shame and guilt still lingered, yet Mother, Venisi, and I couldn't bring ourselves to talk about it. We each had to figure out a way to deal with our emotions because it was like an unspoken, taboo topic. Rev. Katoanga could not understand why I was so shaken up, but he sensed there was something deeper than what was being discussed.

In light of the urgency of the situation, time was of the essence. I jumped into action, contacted the captain, put together a crew, and got fuel prepared and everything else deemed necessary to make this trip happen. I was at the wharf to ensure the boat had clearance as this was not one of its scheduled trips. All aboard as the engine started and we were ready to pull out. An urgent message came, from the government of Tonga, seeking help with a rescue operation as an S.O.S. call for help from the MV *Takuo* as it capsized between Matuku and Nomuka.

The MV *Lotoha'angana* was already fully loaded, packed with church members, families, and friends alike of the deceased. Having to make an almost impossible choice, I hopped on board and advised the government officials that this voyage would take off as scheduled, and then it would become a rescue mission. But we had to disembark and unload Rev. Selu Mafi's body in Nomuka first and the people that were escorting him before we began the rescue operations. The government officials agreed and they boarded some police officers to come with us and help with the rescue.

The MV *Takuo* capsized as it left Vava'u after a big festivity in celebration of an area conference for the Free Wesleyan Church of Tonga. Many people from Tongatapu, Ha'apai, 'Eua, and Niua boarded ferries to attend this momentous occasion. Hon. 'Akau'ola,

Minister of the Police, was no exception as he sent a choir from the prisoners of *Tolitoli* (Tonga's prison) to sing and represent his jurisdiction. After the celebration, it was time to return. That same day, the small choir of prisoners were gifted with food and Tongan *tapas* (*koloa faka Tonga*) before boarding the *Takuo*, a fishing boat that belonged to the police department, at the Vava'u harbor to head back to Tongatapu.

We arrived at Nomuka facing rough sea conditions, which made the exit process challenging as there was no wharf except an interchanging exit from the MV *Lotoha'angana* to smaller boats over the sea to take the passengers to dry land. The late Rev. Selu Mafi's body was escorted off first in a very dignified manner with great care despite this hurdle. The escorting passengers followed and the last person to exit was Rev. Finau Katoanga. I escorted him personally to the small boat to be taken to land.

As soon as all of the passengers exited the boat, I told the captain there was no time to waste as we were now in a rescue operation responding to an S.O.S. call. I instructed the captain to sail in the southeastern direction. As we got outside of Nomuka, I told the captain we needed to wait it out until dawn, as this area was known for its many reefs, which we were unable to identify in the dark. As soon as daybreak came, we continued onward traveling in the southeastern direction, and there we spotted the *Takuo*. The boat had flipped and overturned.

As we got closer, there was a small boat from 'Uiha at the scene, but they hesitated to turn the *Takuo* boat over before it sank to the bottom of the ocean. I then remembered that there were police officers on board that came with us from Tonga to help with the rescue operations. I asked one of them to jump into the sea with a rope and tie it to the *Takuo* so we could haul the boat over to a nearby island. This was a dangerous task and none of the police volunteered to accept the assignment. I then yelled out to one of the guys on the small boat from 'Uiha to jump and take the rope and he did. This brave young man swam over to the *Takuo*, an extremely dangerous task indeed, and he tied the rope to the boat, which allowed us to haul the overturned boat to an island in Nomuka called Nomu'eiki.

Capsized boat Takuo

Another picture of the Takuo from a different angle

I instructed the police officers to break open the boat. As they did, we found a woman still alive, and in another section they busted open, there was a man and a small child still alive. I considered this a successful rescue mission as we were able to save three lives. The people of Nomuka came to this remote beach area and lovingly covered up the bodies of the dead with *ngatu* (Tongan tapa cloth). I sent out a message to Rev. Finau Katoanga and the rest of the passengers that we would have to leave immediately to escort the bodies of the deceased to Tongatapu. Rev. Katoanga and the rest of the church members all came aboard. We left for Tongatapu and the people of Nomuka later carried out the burial of Rev. Selu Mafi.

The voyage back to Tongatapu was of great sadness. The encounter of an unexpected tragedy connected us all on a human level of deep sorrow. A rescue mission unplanned; as in life, many unforeseen events occur, reminding us of how short life is. I looked out into the ocean as we passed through each wave and my thoughts took me into some unknown place of reflection. My memory flashed back to 1978 when I first received word that my first boat, the MV *Ongo Ha'angana*, capsized in 'Utungake, Vava'u. I remember the first question I asked was whether there were any casualties. As soon as I heard the answer was no, an overwhelming feeling of relief came over me.

I closed my eyes as my heart grieved at the loss of human lives. I felt angry and helpless at the same time. What else could I have done? What do we say to the families of the deceased? These and so many other questions kept rewinding through my mind. I always drew strength from Mother's words, "It is what it is," but this time, the words were neither fitting nor appropriate. Although I knew what she meant, to accept things as they are, but this process is not a one-size-fits-all. It is a personal journey that one must walk through on their own terms, just as the grieving and mourning process is different for each person, and it takes time to heal.

As we approached the Queen Salote Wharf (*Uafu Kuini Salote*), it was packed with people. The boat deck door was lowered, and the police rushed in to remove the dead as so many people wanted to show off that they were part of the rescue mission. I called out a command to close the deck door and no one was to exit the boat until we paid proper respect. Rev. Finau Katoanga started off with a song, and as the passengers on the boat sang, the people standing on the wharf joined in singing. Oh, a melody of sweetness and sorrow, an echo of sadness and praise, a sound so reverent and comforting to the brokenhearted. After the singing, he then offered a somber prayer to console the spirit of the dead and ease the pain of the living. A moment stamped into my memory bank as the first rescue mission of my boat responding to an S.O.S. call from the *Takuo*.

After the song and prayer, the captain of the MV *Loto Ha'angana*, Tautalanoa Leota, waited for me to give my okay before he gave the command to lower the boat's deck. As soon as it opened, the police took the bodies of the dead to the morgue to be identified. The passengers along with the survivors of the *Takuo* then exited the boat. I quietly slipped away from the chaotic scene to retire home as this trip had tested the limits of my patience and made me question so many things in life.

I got home, crawled into bed, and immediately fell asleep out of pure exhaustion. Days after this incident, I awaited an inquiry from the government for us to give an account of the rescue but no inquiry came. Weeks went by and still no inquiry. Months went by as it turned into years and still no inquiry at all. This literally broke my heart as I tried to understand the reasons for this gross negligence by the government. Are they turning a blind eye on purpose? I really don't know nor understand the reason why the government of Tonga did not look into this matter and investigate further. I will leave it at that as it is not my place to question their actions. But out of personal curiosity, I asked this question: did the lives of the dead from the sinking of the *Takuo* not matter? As one human being to another, can we really ignore this tragic event and pretend it did not happen and not hold anyone accountable? Whether the *Takuo* sank because of an accident or some other reason, the very least the government should have done was to provide closure to the families of the deceased.

'Akilisi Pohiva used this sad and tragic incident as one of the many examples to demand transparency from the government as he was a very vocal activist for political reform. I identified with 'Akilisi's position and joined the cause of what he fought for as the government of Tonga needed to be accountable to the people they serve. This idea was very new to Tonga as it had been ruled strictly by the monarchy for over one-hundred-plus years. We both knew this would be a long and difficult battle to fight for reform, but we knew that it is a cause worth fighting for.

The examples and evidence we had collected were mounting up and growing at an alarming rate. As sad and tragic as the sinking of the *Takuo* had been, this incident shook up the people of Tonga to examine the customs and traditions of our country. The people never questioned the government, and if they did, it was never expressed. However, 'Akilisi preached about the principle of democracy where the people should elect their representatives to serve in parliament and allow their voices to be heard. This incident caused the pro-democracy movement to gain traction and pushed the Tongan people to question this long-held feudal monarchy government.

To date, the government of Tonga still has not made any inquiry concerning the sinking of the *Takuo*, thus leading me and so many other people to draw our own conclusion based on what we witnessed. My guess is probably as good as anyone else's. Why? As I mentioned before, I will not venture to understand the government's position and the reasoning for the lack of interest in this matter. But loss of human life is not something to be taken lightly. Without transparency, without any proper acknowledgment, without any accountability, without any inquiry, there is no closure, not only for the souls of the dead so they may rest in peace, but more so for the living, the family of those that are gone forever.

    This incident was a wakeup call for me to continue to expand my ferry boat service so that it could provide transportation needs and also serve to rescue boats at sea. It became clear that the government lacked resources even on an emergency basis. It was a sad day to acknowledge the huge gap between the people's needs and the government's response. I could not point fingers at anyone to change things, but I told myself to be the change I wanted to see.

Chapter 15

Deep Roots

Story Behind the Story

Nothing can quite capture the spirit of the Tongan people more than the words of the motto of our national seal coat of arms: "Koe 'Otua mo Tonga ko hoku Tofi'a" ("God and Tonga are my Inheritance"). This grand design Sila 'o Tonga (Seal of Tonga) came about under the leadership of King Siaosi Tupou I as he brought the three dynasties together, the lineage of the kings of Tonga, namely the Tu'i Tonga, Tu'i

Tonga Code of Arms--Koe Sila 'o Tonga.
Iimage courtesy: https://en.wikipedia.org/wiki/Coat_of_arms_of_Tonga

Ha'atakalaua, and the Tu'i Kanokupolu. Under this unification act, Tonga was now a united nation under the reign of King Siaosi Tupou I. In 1875, he masterminded, founded, and established the first formal government and constitution as well as the coat of arms. (Wikipedia, history of tonga, 2022)25

The essence of the rich heritage of Tonga is captured in the ancient way of oral storytelling handed down from one generation to another. The preservers of history, besides parents and teachers, are church ministers and elders of families or clans sharing verbally the accounts of their memories and stories that they themselves heard directly from their elders. A broader perspective of history is captured by Tongan orators called *punake* (poets and composers), a title given to a person who is supremely talented in the performing arts of orating, singing, and choreography (wikipedia, Lakalaka, 2022)[26].

Tasked with the responsibility of telling and preserving stories through spoken words, lyrics, music, and dancing, a *punake* takes great pride in the crafting and weaving of poetry about the fragrant flowers of Tonga or a place of origin, singing the praises of the monarchy, etc.... The punake uses *heliaki* (metaphors) such as *lau kakala, lau hohoko, lau tu'unga* to stipulate a deeper meaning to their composition specific to the occasion being celebrated, and a *punake*'s talent is judged at the *Pangai* (the festivity grounds of the event taking place).

Equally as important is the carrying out of Tongan traditions, which are done through ceremonial events as people come together to celebrate milestones in life. From birthdays to weddings, academic accomplishment to a religious award, family reunions to school alumni's gatherings. As these events take place, whether it is in our homeland or in our diaspora's foreign locations, wherever Tongans are gathered, they reinforce our customs and our traditions.

The most significant custom is the kava ceremony, which plays an integral part in every aspect of the Tongan society. From an informal faikava circle to an event such as a funeral procession,

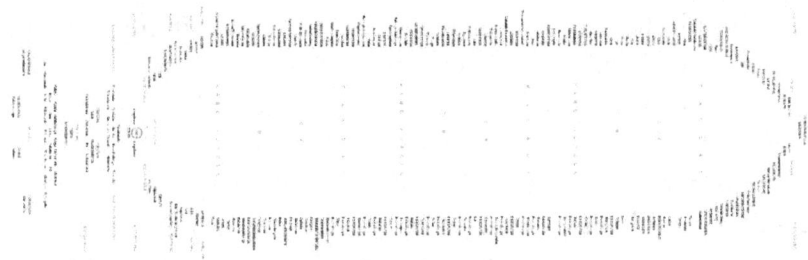

Royal Kava Ceremony Circle

Image courtesy: https://en.wikipedia.org/wiki/Tongan_Kava_Ceremony-Taumafa_Kava

to the most elaborate Taumafa Kava (the Royal Kava Ceremony), the kava ceremony is the pinnacle of our Tongan society. These sacred responsibilities are handled only by ha'a matapule (Chiefly Spokesman) and Nima Tapu (Royal Undertakers).

> "Tongan kava ceremonies play an integral part of Tongan society and governance. Ranging from informal "faikava" or kava "parties" to the highly stratified, ancient, and ritualized Taumafa Kava, or Royal Kava Ceremony, Tongan kava ceremonies continue to permeate Tongan society both in Tonga and diaspora, strengthening cultural values and principles, while solidifying traditional ideals of duty and reciprocity, reaffirming societal structures, and entrenching the practice of pukepuke fonua, or tightly holding on to the land, a Tongan cultural ideal to maintain, preserve, and live traditional Tongan culture". (wikipedia, Tongan Kava Ceremony-Taumafa Kava, 2021)[27]

Through this preservation of customs, in the Kava Ceremony, it keeps the rich tradition of our island nation alive and well in the hearts of every Tongan. An ancient saying claims, *"Tonga mo'unga kihe loto,"* meaning there are no mountains in Tonga except for the hearts of its people. Because of the significant role the *Matapule* plays in the Tongan culture, these orators take great pride in this honorary title, and the way they talk and present themselves in the *Pangai,* or their field of responsibility, are how legends are told and handed down through storytelling.

Unlike the *punake*, where the title is given based on talents, the *Ha'a Matapule* is an honorary title bestowed only by the king and/or his nobles. Once that title is bestowed, that person will have the *Matapule* title indefinitely when performing any duties and will be respectfully addressed by that title. *Matapule* comes with great responsibility, especially in a formal kava ceremony, as every chief in attendance knows his place in the seating arrangement. The ritual of presenting gifts is acknowledged and counted as well as praised publicly during the ceremony.

In every opening of a ceremony, a ritual of *fakatapu* (an acknowledgement of praise as a formal bow down to the Most High, God Almighty, King of Kings, and Lord of Lords) is presented. Immediately following, an orator will usually say something like this: *"'Oku ou kole pe keu hufanga atu 'ihe talamalu 'oe fonua..."* ("I ask to take refuge within the legendary solemn story of our land..."); then he would say, *"Tapu mo'..."* and name the ranking from the highest beginning with the King (*Fale 'o Ha'a Moheofo*) and the royal family down to the nobles and on through the ranks until all clan chiefs are named.

I do not by any means claim to be an expert in the history of Tonga. I only hope to share the knowledge that I have gained through stories handed down to me by my *fanga kui* (grandparents), and through my own experience tell *hoku hala fononga* (the pathway of my journey). For one must understand their identity of who they are and where they come from, in order to have a sure foundation (*maka tu'unga*) to keep us grounded.

Tracing the history of my family lineage, my connection to my ancestors and the land (*fonua*) has deep roots. They are the values that I hold dear and which are anchored by my faith in God, thus forming my beliefs, my aspirations, and the core values of my identity.

To give a *puipui tu'a* (backdrop) to the origin of these deep-rooted beliefs, one must look back to the past to understand the present. During the 19th century, the imperial powers of the world were highly active in acquiring and annexing new countries, and the Pacific was no exception. America had claimed part of Samoa and Britain colonized Fiji. There was anxiety among the emerging Tongan leadership that our island would be colonized by one of the foreign empires.

King Siaosi Tupou I
Image courtesy:
https://en.wikipedia.org/wiki/George_Tupou_I

As ancient tales have it, a meeting was held at a place in Pouono, Vava'u. King Siaosi Tupou I (wikipedia, Tongan Kava Ceremony-Taumafa Kava, 2021)[28] and the chiefs gathered to discuss the imminent threat of colonization. Some chiefs had suggested that some European powers be the protector of Tonga. After listening and taking into consideration the chiefs' suggestion, King Siaosi Tupou I said, "I would like Tonga to be protected, but only by God." He then commenced a *fono* (a public declaration) as he gathered an assembly of chiefs and people and acted out the *tuku fonua*. The King knelt down, took a handful of soil, and threw it up into the air and that was his act of consecrating the land to God. He uttered these words in a solemn prayer: *"God, our Father, I offer unto you my land and my people, and all those who follow after me; I offer them to be protected from Heaven."*

This defining moment in 1839 is the single most celebrated historical event that is deeply rooted in every Tongan's heart, and thus the story of the *Tuku Fonua* (Tuku fonua : the land given to God, 2019) (Tuku fonua : the land given to God, 2019)[29] (giving the land to God) originated. It still evokes an insurmountable sense of pride as all Tongans embrace it with deep respect as it is the cornerstone of our Tongan culture. It was also at this historical event that he articulated the first rule of law, known as the Vava'u Code of 1839. This symbolic act was the foundation of Taufa'ahau's leadership and established a rule of law. When he became the Tu'i Kanokupolu in 1845 and the King to all of Tonga, he expanded the Vava'u Code to the 1850's code of laws and then to the 1862 code of laws, where he included an emancipation edict freeing all commoners of all bondage to the chiefs. Finally, he gave his people a full constitution in 1875.

"Taking refuge in the sacred narratives of our past" refers specifically to the giving of the land to God. Nothing sparks the patriotism, loyalty, honor, and pride that penetrates the hearts of the Tongan people more than the telling and retelling of the story of the *Tuku Fonua*. The wisdom and heroic act of King Siaosi Tupou I to give Tonga to the God of Heaven and Earth to be the guardian and the protector of its people was exemplary of true faith. The spirit of the *Tuku Fonua at Pouono* (a national treasure) is anchored by a deep sense of faith and spirituality embraced by our ancestors and portrayed in the words of our national anthem, whose words are an actual prayer:

> 'E 'Otua Mafimafi   Oh, Almighty God
> Ko homau 'Eiki koe   You are our Lord
> Ko Koe falala'anga   It is You, the pillar
> Moe 'ofa ki Tonga   And the love to Tonga
> 'Afio hifo 'emau lotu   Look down on our prayer
> 'A ia 'oku mau fai ni   That is what we do now
> 'O Ke tali homau loto   And may You answer our wish
> 'O Malu'i 'a Tupou   To protect Tupou
> (Ko e fasi 'o e tu'i 'o e 'Otu Tonga, 2022)[30]

I am deeply moved by this national solemn prayer as we continue to this day to live by the foundation laid by our ancestors. I acknowledge that with time, waves of changes are to be expected as change is necessary and the only constant in life as we evolve. But I am proud to say that Tonga as a society has not forgotten these spiritual guiding principles of our culture. As we still reserve the Sabbath as a day of rest and all businesses are closed. It is a day dedicated to God as we revere Him as the creator and the protector of our country, and we still honor that tradition even into the twenty-first century.

Her late Majesty Queen Salote Tupou III, (File:Salote Tupou III of Tonga in coronation robe-crop, 2020)[31] a supreme punake,

Queen Salote in her coronation robe Oct 11, 1918
Image courtesy:
https://en.wikipedia.org/wiki/S%C4%81lote_Tupou_III

shared her wisdom through her poetry, and in one of her ta'anga (lyrics) of her composition. She outlined our spiritual heritage represented by the four golden pillars of Tonga, which are also the four core values of our society. They are Fefaka'apa'apa'aki (mutual respect), Feveitokai'aki (sharing and fulfillment of mutual obligations), Lototo (humility and generosity), and Tauhi Vaha'a (loyalty and commitment).

When I grew up, I witnessed these four pillars in my own family, both spoken and unspoken, and I relate to them all in a very personal way. I remember the incident when Mother took Venisi and me to a stranger's house, stood outside, and called out for help. She said, "'Oku ou lele mai mo hoku ongo ki'i 'uhiki...", 'uhiki meaning "little animal," which is a derogatory term used by commoners to refer to their children to convey a deep sense of humility. This type of verbiage is not demeaning or a put-down but is actually a sign of humility at its core as commoners acknowledge the different levels of classes in our society, therefore showing a deeper sense of respect in formal communication.

As I embarked on my own hala fononga (journey), the Tongan culture was deeply rooted in my heart as it was the guiding principle of my life. Looking back at my past, it makes sense of the present and gives me hope for the future generations of my family. Now that I am in my eighties, I have come to appreciate the totality of my experiences for they make up who I am.

My strength came from my firm belief that I was destined to be the provider of my family. My relentless will to succeed stemmed from poverty and lack. The experiences of feeling hopelessness and abandonment were so raw that they drove me to live by my motto: "Failure is not an option." The memory of my mother and her determination to put me through school as the way out from our impoverished situation ignited a fire within my heart that often pushed me beyond my ability. The memory of how I robbed my brother Venisi of an opportunity for him to go to school was like fuel to the fire that already burned inside my heart.

All my experiences, the good, the bad, and the ugly, have contributed to my life as a whole. As Job said in the bible, "...shall we receive good at the hand of God and not adversity...?" (JOB kings james version chapter2 verse10, 2001)[32] This truth penetrates my soul and enlightens my mind to not dwell in the difficulty of the situation but to enjoy the journey. As the book of Ecclesiastes profoundly states, "To everything there is a season, and a time to every purpose under the heaven." (Ecclesiastes king james version chapter3 verse1, 2001)[33]

I reiterate what I said earlier; I dedicated this chapter to tell the puipui tu'a (the backdrop) of my Tongan culture as a pattern emerged throughout my journey that reflects the story behind the story, my foundation built on deep-rooted principles. I carry pride in my heart and I wear it as a badge of honor for my country and my heritage. These deep roots were the anchor of my life, both personally and professionally. They provided a sense of purpose and clarity as I connected the dots back to my great ancestors and the founding fathers of our island kingdom.

The storytelling method (orators) was how our Tongan history passed down through generations. Although variations of concepts, facts, and other elements may differ slightly, the core of the history of Tonga is well known and stays alive in the hearts of its people. The sense of pride, the feeling of patriotism, respect for the land, loyalty to our heritage, and pure love that I have for my Tongan people, especially those from my homeland of Ha'apai, are deep rooted, such that I feel it with every fiber of my being, all the way to my bones, a feeling that words cannot fully express.

Chapter 16

Political Arena

A Public Servant—Voice for the Voiceless

Ten years had elapsed since first becoming a public servant as I exited the political arena in the 1980s. My hands were full dealing with various aspects of my businesses as they had grown expeditiously. I justified my absence with these reasons and I convinced myself to accept such a mediocre excuse. However, as time ticked away, I could no longer ignore these promptings. In moments of stillness, an emergence of self-reflection encompassed my thoughts. A sweeping feeling of emptiness slowly eroded the consciousness of my soul, and I had no choice but to explore the unavoidable question, "What is missing in my life?"

The quick and easy answer would be nothing. I ignored it, justifying that I was passing through, or a midlife crisis, maybe? However, the enchanted allure was not in the frequency of this thought, but in the depth thereof. It caused me to stop and take notice of the waves of feelings flooding the gateway of my heart. As I examined the basis of my emotions, I was forced to open my Pandora's box that I had sealed long ago.

Although I was not quite sure what my Pandora's box would reveal, it was a necessary journey to unravel the source of my unfulfilled heart. It always led me back to that single experience that laid the foundation of my life at the beach at age four. From there, I followed the crumbs of my path throughout my childhood to adolescence to becoming a father, a grandfather, and now at this stage in my life, an entrepreneur businessman. As I peeled away the layers, it revealed how far off I had steered away from my passion, that innate feeling of love for the people of my homeland of Ha'ano, Ha'apai.

This rekindled recollection beckoned a persuasion of self-acceptance. Was this a façade, a pretense of goodwill, or maybe a veneer illusion of benevolence? Asking hard questions to induce personal reflection was a necessary task to rummage through the past, tune out the noises of the world, and allow my soul to reconnect to my moral compass. It reawakened a sleeping giant from within. Talk about a wakeup call. This was a testament to the language of the heart as it hears the echo of the past, a still, small voice, yet powerful like thunder.

At the peak of my career, choices spread out before me, politics, or business. I chose to embrace both to expand my businesses and at the same time take on the responsibility of being a public servant. Once I reached that critical decision, the rest was history.

I traveled back to Ha'ano and all over the Ha'apai Group to see and hear firsthand the source of their grievances. Time and time again, their stories exposed the lack of resources they encountered.

'Uliti Uata—his early years in business

They were not requests for luxury, but rather basic needs such as access to clean water, roads, decent jobs, education, transportation, farming equipment, export and import of agriculture, fishery, etc. It became apparent to me that the people's needs were widespread and help must be rendered from the central government to mitigate the situation. I knew that I must get engaged and involved in politics for me to make any impact on the lives of the people I love so dearly.

This was yet another defining moment as I reconnected to my roots and renewed my vow to represent the people and ensure their voices were heard by those in power. I campaigned in 1990 and won the parliamentary seat as a representative of Ha'apai 13th District. And in 1991, I re-entered the political arena with a rejuvenated spirit, renewed commitment, and optimism.

I met Honorable Samuela 'Akilisi Pohiva, a constituent in parliament (*Falealea*) who later became one of my dearest friends.

Hon. Samuela 'Akilisi Pohiva—16th Tonga Prime Minister Image courtesy:https://upload.wikimedia.or g/wikipedia/commons/thumb/2/24/ Akilisi_Pohiva_ITU_2016.jpg/330px-Akilisi_Pohiva_ITU_2016.jpg

He was a fearless soul and an outspoken advocate with an unapologetic approach for a more democratic system of government. He was driven by his belief to shift the power to the people. He entered the political scene with a vision to implement democracy as a basis for government with accountability to the people it serves. From the very beginning, he spoke candidly and openly as he birthed and nurtured this idea. He single-handedly took on the government as a crusader for the poor and the most vulnerable. 'Akilisi had unparalleled conviction as he made it his mission and life's purpose to help poverty-stricken people and the neglected in our society. He fought tirelessly with a resolute passion, unyielding aggressiveness, a zeal for equality, all of which was powered by his love for the Tongan people.

In December 2013, Parliamentarians for Global Action presented him with their annual Defender of Democracy Award, in recognition of his three and a half decades of campaigning for greater democracy in Tonga. He was the first Pacific Islander to receive the award.[23] (Wikipedia, Akilisi Pōhiva, 2022)[34]

His passion, aligned with my burning desire to speak for the voiceless and defend the rights of the forgotten, connected us like magnets. We immediately bonded like brothers. This cause was so deep and personal that it attracted 'Akilisi and me to join forces. We fought side by side to bring about pro-democracy, a reform to a century-old political system of constitutional monarchy.

This idealistic concept of a functioning government for the people and by the people was a seed that 'Akilisi planted and it had taken root. Although it was only a sprout, it had indeed shown life. The message began to echo throughout parliament, beyond the walls of the legislative house, and onto the judicial and the executive branches. 'Akilisi told me, "'Uliti, you take on the economic reform and I will take on the political reform." We divided and conquered by using our individual strengths from our respective field of expertise. We continued with the help of so many people that it is too long of a list to name them all.

Some key figures played a significant role in the establishment of this political reform movement, such as 'Amanaki Havea, Patele Sio Finau, and Futa Helu. There were also other representatives that pushed the work forward, such as Laki Niu, Finau Tutone, Uili Fukofuka, Siosiua Liava'a, Simote Vea, and Semisi Tapueluelu to name a few. The message began to spread like wildfire and more and more people joined the fight. It sparked a public outcry for more transparency as 'Akilisi exposed a history of misconduct and corruption. From contempt for reporting on the parliamentary proceedings, to written articles alleging the monarchy's secret fortune, to several charges of sedition where he landed himself in prison on many occasions, 'Akilisi stood his ground time and time again like a majestic redwood tree, immovable and undeterred. He embraced the difficult journey ahead, a battle and sacrifice he willingly accepted at any cost.

> Monday, April 27, 1998 - 10:40 "Member of Parliament, 'Akilisi Pohiva, was acquitted on two charges of defaming King Taufa'ahau Tupou IV, which were brought against him by the Crown. The charges followed an interview of 'Akilisi Pohiva by Michael Ybarra of the American Wall Street Journal." (Akilisi acquitted on defamation charges, 1998)[35]

> Saturday, August 30, 2003 - 10:00 "'Akilisi Pohiva, the controversial, Tongatapu no. 1 People's Representative to the Tongan parliament won his most serious court battle ever when a jury cleared him and his associates on May 19 on charges of crimes against the state." From Matangi Tonga Magazine Vol. 18, no. 2, August 2003. (Jury clears Pohivas in sedition trial, 2003)[36]

Civil unrest began to sweep across the country. Frustration and anger began to mount, caused by slow progression over public demand for transparency and the ongoing distrust as the government's patterns of corruption came to light. People gathered in large groups and in public spaces, calling and demanding for political reform, but to no avail. Many requests had been formally submitted to the palace and the prime minister but still no movement or actions. Political rallies were organized where 'Akilisi and I, along with other key leaders of the pro-democracy movement, led the crowd through the capital of Nuku'alofa backed by thousands of protestors as we walked side by side, joining hands to display unity and solidarity in our demands for political reform. We marched to the palace's office and I delivered the *tohi tangi*

Pro-Democracy Leader's Movement

Reform Leaders Marching hand in hand to show UNITY & SOLIDARITY

(petition letter) to Ma'afu Tukuiaulahi, which stated the people's demand for political reform.

In 2005, government employees started an organized union in a united effort demanding an increase in pay. The government set aside a budget to accomplish this task but failed to deliver on their promises due to a mismanagement of funds. They provided a sixty-percent increase to top-level positions while the middle and lower-ranked employees received nothing. Their anger and frustration brewed over and they performed the biggest walkout in the history of Tonga. The people's demand was for a sixty-percent increase in pay for high-level positions, seventy-percent increase in pay for mid-level positions, and eighty-percent increase in pay for lower-level positions.

'Uliti Uata at the palace handed to Lord Ma'afu people's grievance letter

From the political spectrum, we heard, understood, and felt the people's anguish over this matter. So, as politicians we intervened and took on the people's demand for better pay, which forced the government to act. Eventually, the government agreed to the people's demand and the pay increase happened in 2005. Here is an excerpt from *Matangi Tonga* on covering this event: "Tonga's civil servants decide to continue strike."

> Submitted by Letters to MTO on Friday 12 August 2005 10:15am
>
> PSA and the march
>
> In a first of its kind, Civil Servants have openly and publicly criticized their heads of departments (Level 1), Cabinet and the Privy Council. They don't agree with government's approach to the public sector reform. They don't agree with the figures from the Minister of Finance and his Secretary. They have collectively walked out of their work stations. They ignored Cabinet's call for all to return to work and make use of the existing mechanisms to address their

grievances. They ignored Privy Council's decision that their demands cannot be met. They have rejected Cabinet's good will and conciliatory offers of 12.5%, 10-5-20 and the sweeteners for the teachers and health workers. (Tonga's civil servants decide to continue strike, 2005)[37]

It was now 2006, the pro-democracy movement entered its fifteenth year, and the government had not budged one bit.

King Taufa'ahau Tupou IV
Image courtesy:
https://en.wikipedia.org/wiki/T%C4%81ufa%CA%BB%C4%81hau_Tupou_IV

September 10th of the same year, the country went into mourning, grieving the loss of our beloved king, His Majesty King Taufa'ahau Tupou IV. He ruled the country and reigned for forty-one years after he took the crown in 1965 following the death of his mother, Queen Salote III. The royal family had ruled with absolute power over the Kingdom of Tonga since 1845.

On November 16th, 2006, a pro-democracy political rally gathered at Pangai (city park) in the capital of Nuku'alofa as they anxiously awaited parliament's

Prince Ata, Tupouto'a-Lavaka, and 'Ulukalala in mourning attire for Tupou IV
Image courtesy:
https://upload.wikimedia.org/wikipedia/commons/thumb/a/a5/Tonga_princes.jpg/330px-Tonga_princes.jpg

decision on democracy. As hours ticked away, the crowd became more anxious as the Legislative Assembly of Tonga was due to adjourn for the year. Despite promises of action, they had largely ignored the people's outcry for democracy and made little progress to further this agenda in the government. 'Akilisi and I pressured the legislature for an open dialogue to at least discuss the people's concerns regarding political reform, but to no avail. 'Akilisi told me to only focus on the chair

March leaders, from left Lepolo Taunisila, Vili Kaufusi, 'Akilisi Pohiva, 'Uliti 'Uata, and Clive Edwards. Nuku'alofa, 1 June 2006. Photo Linny Folau /Image courtesy: Matangi Tonga

and pressure him to allow a platform for a discussion while he focuses on other avenues. Toward the afternoon hours, it became apparent that it had come to a deadlock as the chair of parliament flat-out refused our request.

Thursday, June 1, 2006 - 16:23. Updated on Sunday, March 10, 2019 - 17:58.

Over a thousand people took to the streets of Nuku'alofa today, in a national march to present to the Palace a letter of petition calling for "political reform".

The march from the Nuku'alofa school grounds to Pangai Lahi began after the Tongatapu high schools marched for the opening of parliament. Timed for lunch time so that civil servants would be free to join the march, the main part of the crowd gathered at the old Vaiola grounds while another group started from the Teufaiva area.

It was led by the People's Representatives and members of the People's National Committee for Political Reform, including 'Akilisi Pohiva, 'Isileli Pulu, William Clive Edwards, Vili Kaufusi, Sunia

Fili, 'Uliti Uata and Lepolo Taunisila, and followed by other supporting groups such as the Public Service Association, People's Democratic Party, Tonga Human Rights and Democracy Movement, the Tonga National Business Association, the Council for the Farmers, Friendly Island Teachers Associations and others (Tongan protest marchers call for political reform, 2006)[38]

'Akilisi and I slowly made our way toward the crowd with a look of vanished hope written all over our faces as we had exhausted all possible avenues available to us. With no light at the end of the tunnel, we both could not speak any words of comfort to the people who had so much yearning for a political reform. Instead of addressing the crowd, we sat in the center with our heads bowed in silence, a sign of total defeat. This was our way of saying to the people, "We have done everything within our power and we have failed you. We now pass the baton over to you, the people of Tonga, as we have come to the end of our reach."

This was the tipping point as people's anger boiled over like an old wound bursting open with blood gushing out uncontrollably. They expressed their frustration over loudspeakers, and in an instant, around midafternoon, the peaceful rally erupted into an evening of widespread lawlessness and mayhem. The crowd went wild as the people took to the streets of Nuku'alofa rampaging through businesses and burning down buildings.

Riot in Tonga—Nov 16, 2006
Image courtesy:
https://en.wikipedia.org/wiki/2006_Nuku%CA%BBalofa_riots

The 2006 Nuku'alofa riots, also known as the Tongan riots,[1] started on 16 November, in the Tongan capital of Nuku'alofa. The Legislative Assembly of Tonga was due to adjourn for the year and despite promises of action, had done little to advance democracy in the government. A mixed crowd of democracy advocates took to the streets in protest. The riots saw a number of cases of robbery, looting, vehicle theft, arson, and various property damage. (Wikipedia, 2006 Nukuʻalofa riots, 2022)[39][z]

Marchers at Pangai Lahi, Nuku'alofa, 1 June 2006— Image courtesy: Matangi Tonga

Marchers next to the Royal Palace Nuku'alofa today. Nuku'alofa, 1 June 2006— Image courtesy: Matangi Tonga

Marchers arrive at Pangai Lahi next to the Royal Palace. Nuku'alofa, 1 June 2006.—Image courtesy: Matangi Tonga

The prime minister ordered 'Akilisi and me be brought before him. As we came face-to-face, he asked us, "What is it that you want?"

Our answer was simple and direct: "The people of Tonga want political change."

Prime Minister Feleti Sevele agreed, wrote a letter, and signed his approval for the change. We took the document to the people and I stood up before the crowd and read the letter aloud. Afterward, we encouraged the people to disburse and retire to their homes as the government had agreed to their demand for political change. Some representatives of the people and I went together to the A3Z, Tonga's radio station, and made a public announcement calling the people to end the riot and restore order to the country. Both 'Akilisi and I were charged with sedition, along with other pro-democracy leaders, but we were acquitted later, and all charges were dropped. "In 2007, Uata was one of several pro-democracy MPs charged with sedition over speeches given before the 2006 Nuku'alofa riots.[4] The charges were dismissed in September 2009".[5] (Wikipedia, Uliti Uata, 2022)[40]

Hon Samuela 'Akilisi Pohiva
image courtesy:
https://ast.wikipedia.org/wiki/%CA%BBAkilisi_Pohiva

Three days before his coronation on August 1, 2008, King Siaosi Tupou V graciously announced that he would relinquish most of his power and the day-to-day operations over to the prime minister. The king also announced that there would be parliamentary reform in the 2010 elections. The sovereign of the kingdom voluntarily surrendered his powers to meet the democratic aspirations of his people as he too favored a more representative-elected parliament.

King Siaosi Tupou V
Image courtesy: 2011
https://en.wikipedia.org/wiki/George_Tupou_V

The Tongan Legislative Assembly was established following the 2010 election, the first under a new system that saw the majority of seats elected by national suffrage. The number of people's representatives in parliament increased to seventeen out of the twenty-six available seats, which left nine for the nobles. A victory indeed. The Taimi Media Network described it as "Tonga's first democratically elected Parliament."

After the 2010 election, Tu'ivakano was the prime minister and he appointed 'Akilisi Pohiva to be the minister of health. On the 25th of January 2011, 'Akilisi resigned from his post. The prime minister appointed me as Tonga's minister of health. I served in this position for more than a year until I resigned on July 30th, 2012, due to health issues. 'Akilisi went on to be Tonga's prime minister in 2014 and again in the 2017 election until his passing on the 12th of September 2019.

The Tonga Broadcasting Commission reported on January 18th, 2018: "Prime Minister Hon. 'Akilisi Pohiva read out the list of Cabinet Ministers who he appointed and finalized and approved by His Majesty King Tupou VI." Among his appointees was the Minister of Commerce, Trade, and Labour, my son, Honorable Dr. Tevita Tu'i Uata.

Hon. Dr Tevita Tuʻl Uata—Minister of Commerce, Trade and Labour

His action surprised many as 'Akilisi always operated under a strict moral and ethical code. 'Akilisi was criticized as though he acted against his own rules and appointed a non-elected member to the cabinet. When asked to justify his appointees, 'Akilisi defended his action and stated, "…Besides his educational background, Dr. Tu'i Uata was picked because of his gifts and his talents." This was a great honor as I felt the trust 'Akilisi had for my son to carry on the legacy of being a public servant.

Dr Tevita Tu'i Uata is a Tongan politician and former Cabinet Minister. He is a member of the Democratic Party of the Friendly Islands.[1] He is the son of former MP 'Uliti Uata.[2] (wikipedia, Tevita Tu'i Uata, 2020)[41]

On 25 August 2017 King Tupou VI sacked Pohiva and dissolved the Assembly and called fresh elections in the hope of getting a more tractable Prime Minister.[32][33] The resulting 2017 Tongan general election was a landslide for the DPFI,[34] and Pohiva was re-elected as Prime Minister, defeating former Deputy Prime Minister Siaosi Sovaleni 14 votes to 12.[35] His post-election Cabinet included one Minister from outside the legislative assembly, Dr Tevita Tu'i Uata.[36] (Wikipedia, Akilisi Pōhiva, 2022)[42]

Hon. 'Uliti Uata & Hon. 'Akilisi Pohiva in 2010—*image courtesy: Matangi Tonga*

I served a total of twenty-nine years and 'Akilisi served thirty-plus years in the political arena. I worked side-by-side with my dear friend as public servants, and we journeyed together through thick and thin. But all in all, our friendship endured the test of time.

I speak with great reverence the name of my dear friend. The people's hero, a commoner who defied the tradition of our profoundly hierarchical society and became Tonga's prime minister (highest position in the government aside from the king himself). Samuela 'Akilisi Pohiva, your name now written in history, revered and admired, and will be remembered for generations to come as "Tonga's Father of Democracy."

Tonga's Prime Minister Hon Samuela 'Akilisi Pohiva (78) was laid to rest today, September 19, 2019, at the Telekava Cemetery, Kolomotu'a—image courtesy: Matangi Tonga

Love him or hate him, one cannot deny he was a visionary man with conviction and purpose. I bow down to you with great humility and utmost respect for your civil service. A true people's servant. May you rest in peace as your spirit soars through the sky like an eagle to watch over our land and the people of Tonga. Guard our democracy to safeguard the future of our Island Kingdom and be Tonga's guardian angel from heaven. Until we meet again, my friend.

Chapter 17

Far Reaching

A Life of Service—Paying It Forward

I am a firm believer that you never know how far-reaching an act of kindness can be. I can vouch for the impact acts of kindness had in my own life. In a moment of desperation, a stranger's compassion for our family's circumstances changed my perspective forever. Even from the age of four, my memory of deep sobs and feelings of emptiness is still with me. Remembering how the devastation of poverty subdued our family to walk with our heads bowed in shame and guilt. The snapshot of this moment in time, his kindness illuminated the dark corners of my mind and allowed a ray of sunshine to infiltrate my soul.

I grew up with this unshakable faith that there must be a God. He heard my mother's plea, and the answer to her prayer came through the head of the Lutui family. His hand extended in kindness was a miracle in my young mind. I wanted to mimic his behavior and model my life in a like manner.

I grew up hearing Bible stories talking about how faith is like a mustard seed and so powerful that you can tell the mountain to move and it will obey. (evangelist s. m., Matthew king james version, chapter 17, verse20, 2001)[43] What I believed deep inside to be true was a stark contrast to the outside world I experienced, yet I was not deterred. Story after story in the Bible talked of how Jesus performed miracles, causing the lame to walk, the blind to see, and the mute to talk, to name a few. (evangelist s. m., Matthew king james version, chapter11, verse5, 2009)[44]

Melodies of music are a great source of inspiration, and poetry is painting that picture to come alive with your words. Many years ago, I heard a song titled, *"That's What Faith Must Be"* by Michael Card. (That's What Faith Must Be, 2017)[45] As I re-read the words, it began to resonate with my spirit so I started to formulate my own thoughts of what faith means to me; and soon the words started to rhyme. I knew I must capture my thoughts in a snapshot of time.

> *The seed of faith is but a miracle,*
> *For it is the language of the soul*
> *It seeks the invisible hand you cannot hold,*
> *To guide you through the path you walk.*
>
> *It beckons trust even if you cannot see,*
> *To conquer fear and be set free*
> *And boldly declare your love to Thee*
> *For faith is belief even the mind cannot conceive.*

It made sense now that my faith was birthed at a tender age, which caused this belief to bury deeply into my unconscious mind.

Even when the harsh reality revealed its ugly face and dictated a bleak future, it could not undo the seed that had already been planted. Because I chose faith over fear, I believe in miracles, I believe in possibilities, I believe in kindness, and I believe in the goodness of humanity.

This deep-rooted faith learned at a young age remained constant throughout my life and steadfast like a mighty oak. One of my granddaughters—Melanie—her favorite poem *"The Oak Tree"* (Jr., 2016)[46] by Johnny Ray Ryder Jr, embodies this concept and captures it vividly. The power of this poem spoke volume to my heart, so my daughter Melenaite Uata Sr took liberty and wrote in her own words the inspiration extracted from this poem. She unraveled her own truth as she analyzed lessons learned from the strength of the oak tree.

The Oak Tree's Strength
By Melenaite Uata Sr

The fiery wind blew with great force
The oak tree's leaves snapped and took off
Tamed it's tower with speed and strength
Thinking it will win at the end

But the oak tree remained strong
Held its ground and stood tall
Curious, the wind softly whispered
Oak, how did you withstand such bluster?

The oak tree with confidence replied
You can sway me left or right
Break off my branches with your might
Tear my limbs with tactics fright

Even with your temperament and ferocity
Bring on all you've got, I don't scare easy
Mother earth molded me with great splendor
Majestic and glorious with unmatched cantor

With vitality and strength connected to the earth
The secret lies within my birth
You can't touch them even if you try
They are buried deep inside.

This mindset of extending a helping hand steered my imagination to think of ways to provide service even in my situation of lack and scarcity. My analytical mind reasoned with logic that it is impossible to think of serving others when I can't even help myself. But that did not stop me from imagining a bright future where I can extend a helping hand to someone in need.

In the beginning, when Lu'isa and I started our family, we operated on survival mode. We did anything and everything to be able to support our family. But when the business started to take off, my focus shifted from survival to service. The questions I kept asking were, what can I do to serve others? How can I help my neighbors, my community, and my hometown of Ha'ano? This thought was front and center in all my decision making, the driving force of my inspiration, and the guiding principle of my passion.

Even when I felt defeated, I asked yet another question: what else can I possibly do? After all, I am but one person, and there were days when I felt so small and helpless, my grand ideas vanished into thin air. Now, in my eighties, I have nothing but time on my hands to reminisce through thoughts and ideas that depict my journey and explain some of my actions. One of my daughter's poems was inspired by another poem titled "It's Up to You" (It's Up to You, n.d.)[47] by an unknown author. Her words rang true as she wrote the words in a poetic artform.

"One Hero—YOU"
By Melenaite Uata SR

One word can frame your thoughts
One song can stir up the soul
One seed can spring a flower
One acorn grows to a mighty oak

One smile can make you happy
One friendship gives you strength
One faith can bring up hope
One praise brightens your day

One vote can give you freedom
One ray of sunshine brightens a room
One spark of light subsides darkness
One laughter will change your mood

One step begins your venture
One thank-you conquers prayer
One gratitude will raise your spirit
One act of service can show you care

One voice conveys your power
One heart can feel the truth
One hero can make a difference
And that hero is YOU.

There was a tipping point in time, when I decided to stop overthinking, and made a stand to help. As I crossed paths with people and saw a need, I acted according to the dictates of my heart. Whether the need was great or small, from paying school tuition to providing employment to building homes destroyed by hurricanes to rescuing a family from bankruptcy. The degree of the service rendered varied, but my goal had been the same, to pay it forward so others can experience kindness as I experienced it as a child.

Going beyond individual help, I expanded the same mindset into my business motto, where my main focus was on providing a service according to the needs of the people. From establishing a store to running a taxi service, to the tour guide business, to buses for transportation, to agriculture and exporting, to inter-island air services, to ferry boat routes by sea, to the Liahona Alumni Association, and even my political career, all were established with a goal to serve the people of Tonga. And because I embodied this philosophy as my business model, I have reaped the benefits a hundred-fold.

The Lord truly magnified my ability and allowed my hands to be extended in service of others. The reward was in the simple gestures of gratitude and knowing that I've made an impact in their lives. And the deep concept of service is told in one of my favorite inspirational short stories originally by Loren Eiseley called "The Star Thrower," but it was adapted to this current version:

> "Making a Difference"
>
> One day a man was walking along the beach when he noticed a figure in the distance. As he got close, he realized the figure was that of a boy picking something up and gently throwing it into the ocean. Approaching the boy, he asked, "What are you doing?"
>
> The youth replied, "Throwing starfish in the ocean. The sun is up, and the tide is going out. If I don't throw them in, they'll die."
>
> "Son," the man replied, "don't you realize there are miles and miles of beach and hundreds of starfish? You can't possibly make a difference."
>
> After listening politely, the boy bent down, picked up another starfish and threw it into the surf; then, smiling at the man, he said, "I made a difference for that one." (Wikipedia, The Star Thrower, 2021)[48]

I was once like the starfish that got saved that day. With a heart full of gratitude, I wanted to give back and pay it forward to make a difference in someone else's life. The essence of service is not the act itself but the compelling feeling of benevolence, charity, kindness, and sympathy, which enlarges the dimensions of our hearts and moves us to act in synchronicity with our compassion. With this magnitude of elevated emotions, we are in tune with the frequency of our human connections sending out an electrifying field of energy.

Albert Pine summed up beautifully the far-reaching effect of service when he said, "What we do for ourselves dies with us. What we do for others and the world remains and is immortal." (Wikipedia, Albert Pike, 2021)[49] The depth of the concept of service blesses both the giver and the receiver. As we lift others' burdens, our burdens become lighter. When we extend a helping hand to serve another human being, the Lord blesses our lives in the process as His blessing extends to both the giver and the receiver. The giver feels fulfilled for doing something good, and the receiver is being blessed by receiving the help.

Throughout history, there have been many individuals who chose the road less traveled because they believed in a cause, and they acted according to their deeply held belief. They acted with passion and conviction and their actions changed the course of history. I am awestruck reading about such personalities as the reach of their actions touched millions of lives throughout the world.

Mahatma Gandhi
https://en.wikipedia.org/w/index.php?title=Special:CiteThisPage&page=Mahatma_Gandhi&id=1072359255&wpFormIdentifier=titReform

Gandhi, considered by millions of Indians as the Mahatma ("great soul"), believed in peaceful protest and stood in his conviction of non-violence. He was an anti-war activist with a global legacy as he led millions to a non-violent movement trying to free India from British rule. As noted in his biography, "Every revolution begins with a single act of defiance." (Wikipedia, Mahatma Gandhi, 2021)[50]

Nelson Mandela, after being in prison for twenty-seven years, rose to be a prominent leader and served as president of South Africa from 1994 to 1999. He became the country's first Black head of state and was elected in a fully

Nelson Mandela
https://simple.wikipedia.org/w/index.php?title=Special:CiteThisPage&page=Nelson_Mandela&id=7980472&wpFormIdentifier=titleform

representative democratic election. Mandela was widely regarded as an icon of democracy and social justice, and he received more than 250 honors, including the Nobel Peace Prize. He is held in high regard and deeply respected around the world, but especially in South Africa, where he is often referred to by his Thembu clan name, Madiba, and described as the "Father of the Nation." (Wikipedia, Nelson Mandela, 2021)[51]

"I Have a Dream" is the most iconic speech in American history, delivered by Dr. Martin Luther King, Jr. from the steps of

Dr Martin Luther King
Image courtesy:
https://en.wikipedia.org/w/index.php?title=Special:CiteThisPage&page=Martin_Luther_King_Jr.&id=1072322669&wpFormIdentifier=titleform

the Lincoln Memorial in Washington, D.C. He spoke in front of 250,000 civil rights supporters during the March on Washington for Jobs and Freedom on August 28th, 1963. The speech was a defining moment of the civil rights movement and was ranked the top American speech of the 20th century and has also been described as having "a strong claim to be the greatest in the English language of all time." (Wikipedia, I Have a Dream, 2021)[52] King was an American Baptist minister and activist who became the most notable spokesperson and leader in the American civil rights movement from 1955 until his assassination in 1968. King advanced civil rights through nonviolence and civil disobedience, inspired by his Christian beliefs and the nonviolent activism of Mahatma Gandhi. (Wikipedia, Martin Luther King Jr., 2021)[53]

Mother Teresa was honored in the Catholic Church as Saint Teresa of Calcutta and was considered a living saint. Wearing a simple cotton sari with a blue border, Teresa ventured into the slums of Calcutta. She treated the sick, fed the poor, and founded a school for the underprivileged. She even had to beg for food and supplies to support her mission. Eventually, she

Mother Teresa
Image courtesy:
https://commons.wikimedia.org/w/index.php?title=File:Mother Teresa_090.jpg&oldid=5891660 40

founded the Missionaries of Charity. In her words,

> The foundation shall care for the hungry, the naked, the homeless, the crippled, the blind, the lepers, all those people who feel unwanted, unloved, uncared for throughout society, people that have become a burden to the society and are shunned by everyone. (Wikipedia, Missionaries of Charity, 2021)[54]

Teresa said, "By blood, I am Albanian. By citizenship, an Indian. By faith, I am a Catholic nun. As to my calling, I belong to the world. As to my heart, I belong entirely to the Heart of Jesus."[4] Upon her death on September 5, 1997, she received a state funeral from the Indian government in gratitude for her service to the poor of all religions in the country. Prime Minister of Pakistan Nawaz Sharif called her "a rare and unique individual who lived long for higher purposes. Her lifelong devotion to the care of the poor, the sick, and the disadvantaged was one of the highest examples of service to our humanity."[78] According to former U.N. Secretary-General Javier Pérez de Cuéllar, "She is the United Nations. She is peace in the world."[78] (Wikipedia, Mother Teresa, 2021)[55]

I am mesmerized reading about the histories of these amazing souls as they blessed the lives of millions with their conviction and their actions. They dedicated their lives to the cause they believed in wholeheartedly. They fought vigilantly for justice, peace, freedom, and human rights, as they saw themselves as instruments of service for humanity. As Mother Teresa described her experiences as "a call within a call," she laid the foundation for her legacy by working among the poorest of the poor. She wrote in her diary, "Our Lord wants me to be a free nun covered with the poverty of the cross..." (Spink)[56] She grasped the Bible at its core with this compelling statement and its poignant message regarding human lives, which also resonates with the profound spiritual concept taught in this scripture passage:

> [34] Then shall the King say unto them on his right hand, Come, ye blessed of my Father, inherit the

kingdom prepared for you from the foundation of the world:

35 For I was an hungered, and ye gave me meat: I was thirsty, and ye gave me drink: I was a stranger, and ye took me in:

36 Naked and ye clothed me: I was sick, and ye visited me: I was in prison, and ye came unto me.

37 Then shall the righteous answer him, saying, Lord, when saw we thee an hungered, and fed thee? or thirsty, and gave thee drink?

38 When saw we thee a stranger, and took thee in? or naked, and clothed thee?

39 Or when saw we thee sick, or in prison, and came unto thee?

40 And the King shall answer and say unto them, Verily I say unto you, In as much as ye have done it unto one of the least of these my brethren, ye have done it unto me. (evangelist s. m., Matthew king james version chapter25 verse30, 2001)[57]

To bring this point home, my family and I were the least among our community, and in a crucial moment, we felt the invisible hand of God through the service of a stranger. I am always choked up with deep emotions every time I read this passage, for it stirs up my soul and touches the very core of our humanity.

Chapter 18

Floating Grave

Rescue Mission of MV *Princess Ashika*

In the dead of night, while floating in the midst of the South Pacific Ocean, imminent danger surrounded the MV *Princess Ashika*. Some passengers, mainly women and children, took refuge from the rough sea on the lower deck, unaware of the impending peril. Unbeknownst to the 128 souls on board, they were on a doomed voyage, a catastrophic calamity brewing intensely.

Photograph of MV Princess Ashika pier side at Natovi Landing,. (Ray, 31 August 2008)
Image courtesy:
https://en.wikipedia.org/wiki/File:Princess_ashika.jpg

The ship left Tongatapu on August 5th, 2009, in the late afternoon. Just around midnight, about eighty-six kilometers northeast of the capital of Nuku'alofa, MV *Ashika* began to take on water, then sent out a mayday call followed by a distress beacon. An excerpt of live interaction data captured and taken from a report of the Royal Commission of Inquiry:

> 2.144 At 2350hrs on 5th August 2009, the Coast Watch radio station at Nuku'alofa (Nuku'alofa Radio) logged the following call on the international distress frequency 6215 hertz:
>
> "MAYDAY, MAYDAY, this is Ashika, A3CI2. We are going to sink in this position 20 degrees 24 minutes south, 174 degrees 56 minutes west. (Royal Commission of Inquiry into the Sinking of the MV Princess Ashika, 2010)[58]" (Transport Accident Investigation Commission, 2010)(p74)

"The transmission of this MAYDAY message was the last act of the Master" (p74) right before the boat capsized and sank, taking down with it seventy-four lives, mostly women and children, who were trapped in the enclosed passenger cabin below and had no chance of escape. I cannot imagine the moment these passengers realized they were trapped, and death was inevitable as their lives flashed before their eyes. I cannot begin to fathom the feeling of helplessness as a mother held tightly to her child, knowing this was their last moment together. I cannot wrap my mind around comprehending the pain the families of the victims felt. To have received the news that fateful night that their loved ones were not returning home and whose precious lives were cut short. My deep and sincere condolences go out to those families who are still haunted by this gruesome incident. The vessel now rests on the seabed floor with its precious cargo, a horrific tragedy that brought a nation to its knees.

Just before the stroke of midnight on August 5th, 2009, I was awakened by an emergency alert from the Tonga telegraph and telegram office of a mayday call from the MV *Ashika* ferry. This distressed request by the government was made directly to me as the owner of the Uata Shipping Company, which the MV *Pulupaki* operates under, as they sought assistance with the rescue at sea. I immediately communicated to the MV *Pulupaki* with a stern command to drop everything and proceed immediately to help the passengers and crew of *Ashika*. I was on a radio interacting live during this rescue operation with the captain as well as my two sons who were on board the *Pulupaki* at the time, Dr. Tevita Tu'i Uata as the operational manager and Edward Kay Uata as the chief engineer. I remember feeling sick to my stomach from the shock of this harrowing news compounded by the feeling of helplessness from Nuku'alofa.

I relinquished all authority to my two sons to act using all available resources for this rescue operation as I remained on the edge of my seat, awaiting updated reports. The only help I could render from afar was prayer. I dropped to my knees and poured out my heart with all the sincerity I could muster and with the hope that my cry could reach the heavens. I asked the Lord to show His tender mercy upon *Ashika* and the people on board. About two and a half hours from the initial contact, the MV *Pulupaki* arrived at the scene of the accident. My worst fear was confirmed by the report that the MV *Ashika* had sunk, and many had drowned, but some survived.

Floating Grave

My heart was beating fast as adrenaline rushed through me, and images flashed through my thoughts of the victims as the scale and magnitude of the fatalities unfolded in real-time. I could hear the frenzied noise from the background, but I had confidence in my sons' ability to take control. I remember hearing my son's voice cracking over the radio transmission as he restored order to the chaotic scene. Tu'i yelled out a command from the top deck of the *Pulupaki* in the order of survivors brought on board. "Are there any children survivors? Bring them up first."

Dr Tevita Tu'i Uata

The answer came, "No. No children."

There was a moment of silence; Tu'i took a deep breath and yelled out, "Please tell me if there are any women survivors. Bring them up."

The answer came, "No. No women."

I could feel sadness and pain in my son's voice even over the airwaves when Tu'i's tone lowered and could barely be heard as he asked for a third time, "Are there any elderly survivors? Bring them up."

The answer came, "No. No elderly survivors. The only survivors are men."

The first group of men from the lifeboat boarded, and the *Pulupaki* circled through the area and picked up more survivors from the remaining lifeboats. They reported back to me that it seemed they had gotten all of the survivors, but I did not feel satisfied. I urged them to please make a final round, combing through the area to see if they could spot any more survivors. My instinct proved to be correct as the second time the *Pulupaki* plowed through the waters, they spotted a lifeboat with a single person on top who did not make any motion to indicate if he was alive. They got closer and pulled the man aboard. It was the captain of *Princess Ashika* shivering from the cold and near death, but he barely managed to hang on by a thread. The *Pulupaki* crew immediately stripped off his wet clothes and warmed him up with blankets, and fed him a hot cup of noodles, which managed to save him.

An excerpt taken directly from the Royal Commission Report:

> Nuku'alofa Radio was able to contact the MV Pulupaki, which was following MV Princess Ashika, but some two and a half hours astern, to request her assistance... the MV Pulupaki reached the disaster scene and commenced rescuing survivors. By 04:50 hrs on 6th August 2009, all who survived the sinking had been rescued by the MV Pulupaki. (p6)
>
> 13.54 The Tongan coastal cargo-passenger vessel, MV Pulupaki, was the first vessel at the distress site and rescued all the survivors.
>
> 13.55 It is interesting to note that this vessel underwent a Radio Survey in Nuku'alofa on the 5th of August 2009, the day of the MV Princess Ashika sinking. The H/F (High Frequency) radio was only working effectively on the frequency of 8291kHz...(T 1337).
>
> 3.56 In this instance, the arrangement proved fortuitous as, when Mr. Haseli was called in to keep a watch at Nuku'alofa Radio that same evening due to the illness of the rostered operator, he was able to contact MV Pulupaki on 8291kHz, the frequency which he knew from his visit to the ship earlier in the day, MV Pulupaki would be monitoring, and pass on the MAYDAY message from MV Princess Ashika.
>
> 13.57 The MV Pulupaki reached the site of the sinking at 0231hrs 6th August 2009, and the next vessel to arrive, VOEA Pangai, arrived at 0430hrs 6th August 2009, some two hours later.
>
> 13.58 The MV Pulupaki rescued all the survivors from MV Prince Ashika... (Royal Commission of Inquiry into the Sinking of the MV Princess Ashika, 2010)[59] (Transport Accident Investigation Commission, 2010)*(p609)*

The *Pulupaki* rescue operation was now complete, and they were on their way to Pangai, Ha'apai, with fifty-four survivors on board. This report gave me a sense of relief as my boat was able to help at a critical time of need. Sleep became a burden as I stayed awake for the duration of the night, communicating and helping with directives to both the captain and my sons. I was on the next flight to Pangai, Ha'apai, to greet the survivors, show them support, and aid in any additional way deemed necessary. Looking at the faces of the men that survived, I read silent messages of loss, grief, and despair. They did not rejoice that their lives were spared. They mourned quietly with tears flowing for those that lost their lives at sea. It was an emotional scene, an unforgettable event, to say the least, a difficult time of sorrow that had to be treated with extreme care and respect.

MV Pulupaki

The final report of the Royal Commission of Inquiry into the sinking of the MV *Princess Ashika* was submitted to His Majesty King George Tupou V on the 31st of March 2010. The report was made public for the families of the deceased seeking justice, for the hopeful men and women seeking political reforms, and for the average citizen aspiring for change.

This bona-fide report through the investigative process confirmed long-held distrust of those in power in our tiny island kingdom. Reading through the 630-page verifiable report, frightening, heinous, atrocious, repulsive, and widespread negligence of epic proportions by the government was revealed. It was a field day of public interest exposing abusive power, mismanaged funds, lies, deceits, fraud, forgery, misspent foreign aid, overseas junkets, secret companies, law violations, misrepresentations, unqualified men in positions of trust, and self-serving interest, just to name a few.

An excerpt taken directly from the Report of the Commission confirmed the people's speculation:

> It was scandalous that such a maritime disaster could ever have been allowed to occur. It was a result of systemic and individual failures. (p6)
>
> 8.429 The Chairperson was very frank and honest in her evidence, for example, in her statement that "the tragedy resulted from a failure of the whole Tongan system which struggles with governance and due process of law at all levels" and that in this case, the government failed to carry out due diligence and "procurement policies were not fully complied with when buying the ship" (Exhibit 288 paragraph 7)
>
> 8.430 In her view, the systemic failure was: · The failure in the Ministry of Transport, as responsible for safety issues, failed in issuing a seaworthy certificate for a ship that was unsafe and failed to carry out proper checking of the vessel; · The captain and crew failed to stand up and effectively say that the ship should not sail because it was unsafe; · There was a failure to give passengers adequate warning; · So that the vessel sank because of failure of governance at all levels and sound corporate governance includes commitments and reliance on legislation. (Transport Accident Investigation Commission, 2010) (Royal Commission of Inquiry into the Sinking of the MV Princess Ashika, 2010)[60]

According to *Matangi Tonga*'s analysis, the report places much of the blame for the procurement of the *Princess Ashika* ferry on the cabinet. In the report, the cabinet is cited with pushing the deal through hastily, without sufficient information, and effectively blocking the Procurement Committee and the Anti-Corruption Commission from completing their essential oversight roles. The report went on to describe the Tongan prime minister as defensive in his refusal "to accept the obvious" and his "attempts to deny reality."

The commission dug deep to get to the root cause of the problem, and they left no stone unturned by investigating every correspondence, interaction, meeting, and the paper trail leading up to the tragic event of the sinking of MV *Ashika*. The report identified the former minister of transport, Paul Karalus, as having one of the most "pivotal," "active," and "personal" roles in the tragedy.

The Tongan government faced international censure for its role in purchasing the MV *Ashika* ferry without due diligence. They were scrutinized for approving the purchase of this raggedy boat based on personal opinions, mainly from Paul Karalus, John Jonesse, and Lord Dalgety. Even in Lord Dalgety's own words, he described MV *Princess Ashika* as a "rust bucket" from information he claimed that he became aware of after the sinking. The report also identified that John Jonesse had made "unsubstantiated and inaccurate statements" about the ship being well maintained and seaworthy. The commission describes those statements as "not only patently absurd but dishonest."

The commission's inquiry threw the government into a discombobulated state of bewilderment and disarray as the water got muddier with each finding. The report opened up a can of worms for Tonga, and the government found itself in a complex predicament at the highest level, not to mention the fact that the government paid six hundred thousand Fijian dollars for a boat that sent its people to their final resting place at the bottom of the Pacific Ocean.

In the wake of this spine-chilling incident, the Tongan government also came under scrutiny as the public outcry demanded accountability. The inquiry report described the deaths of the seventy-four victims as "senseless" and the causes of the disaster easily preventable. The report also deemed MV *Princess Ashika* as "unseaworthy" and was in such "appalling condition and that it should never have been purchased." And in Captain Johnson's words, it was "an unsafe ship." (T 2723).

There was clear evidence through this report that the government turned a blind eye and failed to provide due diligence and oversight for the safety of the people they govern. Unlike a natural disaster beyond our control, the sinking of *Princess Ashika* was a man-made disaster. Willie Vi, a lecturer at the Tongan Maritime School and holder of a New Zealand Foreign Ship Masters

Certificate, said, "The vessel was a death-trap. It was like they were just buying a grave. A portable, floating grave." (2022, 2009)[61]

This so-called justice that the Tonga Supreme Court served in the wake of this disaster is absurd. They sentenced three people to prison in April 2011 after finding them guilty of manslaughter by negligence and other charges. It was like a slap on the hand for a serious crime. The government should be ashamed, or at the very least show remorse for purchasing a boat that ended up being a coffin for its people, sealed, nailed, and delivered by the men with abusive authority and driven by greed and power.

> The inquiry later found that *Princess Ashika* had not been surveyed prior to being purchased by the Tongan government and that unfavorable surveys by the Fiji Marine Board were not brought to the attention of the Tongan authorities. A survey was conducted by Tongan Ministry of Transport surveyors on the arrival of the vessel in Tonga. However, despite their subsequent claims that they considered the vessel to be totally unseaworthy, they failed to stop operations of the vessel. (Wikipedia, MV Princess Ashika, 2020)[62]

None of the government cabinet ministers who approved the purchase of MV *Princess Ashika* has been brought to justice. The sinking of the ferry provoked widespread anger as relatives of victims camped for weeks outside the offices of the government-owned Shipping Corporation of Polynesia, which operated the ferry. The *Taimi Tonga* newspaper reported that the government had paid out $80,000 ($45,480 U.S. dollars) to "almost all" the families of those who drowned "in exchange for not pursuing any civil lawsuits against the government."

The reality of this underwater tragedy tormented my mind to question the very fiber that weaves the fabric of our Tongan culture. Has modern Tonga lost connection to its roots? Is the government so corrupt that it is beyond redemption? Do we live in a survival-of-the-fittest and a dog-eat-dog world? Is our island being misled by those in authority with an appetite for power and financial gain? Have the four golden pillars of our society vanished and been replaced by outside influences? Is the very core heritage of being a Tongan blown away by the wind of modernization?

Although the foundation of our society has shifted with the tide of changing times, the root of our Tongan culture lies within the hearts of our people, "koe Tonga mo'unga kihe loto." For it is the heart that renders life and pumps blood to flow through your veins. It is the heart that feels and houses deep emotions. It is the heart that moves you to act and make sacrifices.

Love emerges from the heart and breaks down barriers and conquers all. The heart is the universal language that the blind can see, and the deaf can hear. Quoting a Tongan tradition, when one goes bearing gifts to a celebration or to a funeral, we often say, "Koe me'a fakavale he anga ka koe masiva," meaning, *the gift I present is pale in comparison to the deep love I feel as there is nothing in this world that could express the depth thereof*, which leaves me to conclude that our culture is deeply tied to our country's seal that we pride ourselves in, "God and Tonga are my inheritance."

This was a soul-searching time that led me to battle internally with my thoughts, so I took a step back to reassess my actions and motivation. I grilled myself with hard questions that plagued my thoughts, leaving nothing unturned as I began a full self-evaluation. Why did I render help on behalf of the government when they have attacked me from all angles?

From a political standpoint, I believe in a more democratic process in which the people are empowered to choose their representatives so their voices can be heard. From a business standpoint, I wanted to provide an inter-island ferry service to help with the transportation needs as people are scattered throughout different islands. I thought my business helped the government in this area, but instead, they saw me as a fierce competitor and acted like I was a thorn in their side. They ignored the fact that my business helped the economy by bringing in revenue for the government through taxes. And their biggest oversight was not acknowledging that I provided jobs for the people and the community.

Many powerful men who held key positions in government fought me tooth and nail and fined me with fees, slapped me with lawsuits, and made it exceedingly difficult for me to operate as a businessman. I felt like the story in the Bible of David fighting Goliath as I was a single business owner from the private sector up against the government of Tonga. My fighting spirit was not of vengeance or hatred or even revenge; I fought as a father to put food on the table for my children, and with that mindset, I fought as the patriarch and provider for my family.

The moment I acknowledged humanity at its best and at its worst, the answer became clear. This unfortunate turn of events brought us together, and at that very moment, it was humanity at its best. As the scripture tells us, "…to mourn with those that mourn and comfort those that stand in need of comfort." (Book of Mormon chapter18, 2000)[63]

I realized that I was moved to act because of the deep compassion and love I feel for the people. The love reflected by my sons through their actions on the rescue mission saved fifty-four souls and was a testament that they mimicked what they had seen and witnessed through the path I had paved.

Although the government of Tonga to this day has not extended a token of gratitude or even a simple thank you, I am at peace as I acknowledge my actions were governed by a higher law. The MV *Pulupaki* rendered service the night the *Ashika* sank, and in 1994, the MV *Loto Ha'anaga* rendered service when the *Takuo* sank. Both were rescue missions to save lives, a legacy that I have instilled in the hearts of my children, grandchildren, and great-grandchildren.

I teach the importance of rescuing from a physical, emotional, and spiritual place so that it may become a family tradition carried on even when I leave this world. I want this legacy

Uata Family Photo in July 2010 as we came together for Taki's funeral with only some of the grandchildren and great grandchildren that were present at the time picture was taken

to live on in the hearts of generations to come of the Uata Family. In all things, I return all glory to God. Praise be His name, for He is the King of Kings and Lord of Lords. He is the Alpha and the Omega, the Beginning, and the End. He is a loving God, a merciful God, and the Ruler of the heavens above and the earth below.

Chapter 19

Breaking Point

The Memory of Douglas 'Ofa-ki-Ha'angana Uata

The American theologian Reinhold Niebuhr's famous prayer, "God grant me the serenity to accept the things I cannot change, the courage to change the things I can and the wisdom to know the difference," (Wikipedia, Serenity Prayer, 2021)[64] has been my solace in my darkest hours. These inspired words have soothed my soul and brought comfort to my troubled heart as I accepted it's true that there are things beyond my control.

June 24th, 2010, is a distant memory as over ten years have passed, yet it is still so clear in my mind like it was yesterday. It is as though a hidden passageway has reopened and allowed me to walk back through memory lane. The images are flashing, the soundwaves echoing, the scent permeating, my heart pounding, my pulse racing, and even the bitter taste of sorrow has not dissipated as I recall mourning the loss of my son. There is an old saying that time heals all wounds, but grieving is an individual process. With a heavy heart, I express the emotions of my own experience as I grieved silently. For more than ten years, time has certainly helped ease the pain, but it has not diminished my feelings and the love I feel for my son.

For now, I live with the knowledge that love knows no bounds, and even the very jaws of death are powerless to this phenomenal force. The words of this quote comforted my painful heart: "Death leaves a heartache no one can heal, Love, leaves a memory no one can steal." (Mifflin, n.d.)[65] The depth of love I feel for my son is a timeless treasure that will abide with me forever.

How do I start to unpack the extent of my emotions and free myself from this dismal shadow? My mind evokes more questions than answers as I seek to find the purpose of the untimely death of my son. The words of Washington Irving say it best: "There is a sacredness in tears. They are not the mark of weakness but of power. They speak more eloquently than ten thousand tongues. They are the messengers of overwhelming grief, of deep contrition, and of unspeakable love." (Washington Irving, 2021)[66] It is unnatural for parents to bury their children, but here I am writing from a father's perspective of losing my son.

Soren Kierkegaard once said, "Life can only be understood backwards, but it must be lived forward." (Søren Kierkegaard, 2021)[67] Through these inspirational words, I look back through the lens of time not to dwell on the past but to closely examine my journey. So my story can be understood as I strive to live and move forward with purpose and clarity. Reading through the Bible to find meaning, I discovered this profound truth: "To everything, there is a season and a time to every purpose under the heavens: a time to be born and a time to die, a time to plant and a time to uproot…a time to weep and a time to laugh, a time to mourn and a time to dance."

(Ecclesiastes king james version, chapter3, verse1, 2009)[68] This passage opened and mended my broken spirit to explore God's goodness for He giveth life, and He taketh it away in His own time according to His will.

I began to write down my thoughts as I went deep within to search for the infinite source, the higher power, the divine being, the master intelligence, ruler supreme, and creator of the universe. I expressed my own psalms extracted from the very depth of my soul, as I sing His praises with enlightened insights that have unfolded before me:

> As the light begins to break from the horizon and the warmth of the sun shines through the cloud, it affirms the power of the Almighty.
>
> As the brightness of the stars and other galaxies and the shadow of the moon reflects from the sky, what a testament to His Eternities.
>
> As the hummingbirds singing echoes through the air and the haunting sound of the humpback whales are carried from the deep ocean, what an acoustic heavenly vibe of His divinity.
>
> As the fragrance of the flower blooming with the bees buzzing and the wonderment of nature reflects its glorious beauty, it reminds us of His infinite wisdom.
>
> Hence the birth of a child is but a reflection of God's love, a masterpiece of His creation, as He made us in His likeness and in His Image.
>
> As a son of the Most High, please, oh Lord, hear my plea. Wash away my sins in the blood of Jesus; forgive my iniquities and my unworthiness; redeem my flaws and unrighteous desires; cleanse my mind and purify my heart; make me whole again in Thy presence as I accept my Savior's sacrifice; that He

died on the cross of Calvary for a sinner like me; oh, I stand all amazed of the Omnipotent glory.

I come unto Thee in humility, with a broken heart and a contrite spirit; please, oh Lord, do not hide Thy face from this humble servant; take my hand and lead me on; light the path I walk; awaken my spirit with a fierce conviction of Thy grace; fill my heart with goodness to embrace Thy tender mercy; as the essence of my soul floats freely singing the song of Thy redeeming love.

Oh, my heart is overflowing, and I shall praise Thee in all the days of my life.

From right to left: 'Afa, Lu'isa and Takilesi in the late 1990s

With these reflective thoughts moving around in the confines of my mind, it freed my heart from anger, pain, resentment, sadness, and regret. My mind shifted from the dark corners of hopelessness and into the light, embracing gratitude with euphoria while unveiling precious memories of my son's thirty-three years of his young life.

Douglas 'Ofa-ki-Ha'angana Uata was born a month prematurely on January 30th, 1977, with his twin brother, Arthur, at the UCI Medical Center in Orange, California. He weighed four pounds, and Arthur weighed three pounds. They lived in an incubator at the hospital and were fed with a tube through openings via their heads for a month before they were released home. The translation of Douglas in Tongan is Takilesi, and we called him by his nickname, Taki. It was a miracle they survived the many health challenges they faced, but these twin babies were fighters since birth. Even after they came home, almost every other week, they were back in the hospital due to health complications. But despite all the challenges they faced, the twins fought tirelessly to stay alive through it all.

Taki was number eight and the most obedient child out of my eleven children. He was a deep thinker, and at times, you wondered if he even understood what was being discussed because of his delayed response as he pondered before he spoke. His habit was scratching his head out of frustration when he couldn't express himself or his emotions.

Right to left starting from the back: 'Etuate, Venisi, 'Uliti, Lu'isa, Tu'i, Monisoni and the twins, 'Afa & Taki to in front of our home on Cedar St in Santa Ana, CA

On the flip side, Taki was a joker and used laughter to lighten the mood of any conversation or circumstance. He had such a refreshing sense of humor that it created a space of ease and comfort for everyone around him, but his trademark was making each person he interacted with feel included. He made no judgment against anyone and accepted them unconditionally. And with that gift, he blessed our whole family, friends, colleagues, and even strangers alike.

One such memory attesting to his character still makes me smile to this day. One of my daughters got married, and her American friend Jamie flew from New York to Tonga to attend the wedding. She stayed at our house as a guest, and one afternoon, as we all relaxed on the back porch chatting away and enjoying each other's company, suddenly Jamie jumped up off the floor and onto the couch yelling, "Cockroach, cockroach" while dusting off her clothes, scared for dear life.

Taki picked up the cockroach and said, "You mean this friendly little critter? Oh Jamie, he's harmless. Come meet my friend Jose; he's like family," and we all broke out laughing, especially Jamie.

Taki took the role of guardian and protector of his twin brother. When they were little, each one was assigned a chore to do, and if that wasn't enough, everyone older than the twins called on them to do this and get that. I would hear my wife calling, "'Afa, 'Afa, where are you?"

But here came Taki answering his mother, "I'm coming, Mom," and completed the chore. When his mother made a fuss about 'Afa being lazy and slacking off, Taki would say, "Oh no, Mom. He's doing homework, or he's sleeping," justifying why his twin brother could not answer her call. It got to the point that no one called 'Afa anymore. Everyone just called out Taki's name, and he answered every call without fail.

Taki in middle, 'Afa to right, Soni to left and Lu'isa in front

After high school, Taki went on to trade school to be an electrician. This was the least resistant path to explore as he was incredibly good with his hands, making this move a natural choice. In 2002, Taki flew back to Tonga to prepare for the next phase of his life as he was courting a young lady named

Taki and Lome's Wedding Picture—Jan 2nd, 2003

Salome. January 2nd, 2003, as soon as the government reopened after their holiday leave, Taki and Salome were married.

Taki decided to stay behind in Tonga and gain experience with the ferry boat business I was operating, but he didn't feel it was the right fit. Nine months later, on September 17th, 2003, Taki and Lome flew back to the US. They lived in our home in Santa Ana,

California, while Taki returned to complete his schooling. Once he obtained his certificate as a licensed electrician, Taki and Lome left for Seattle, then on to Hawaii as they followed his career path. Their first child was born July 5th, 2004, and he was named after my grandfather and included his father's middle name, Walter 'Ofa-ki-Ha'angana Uata.

On November 20th, 2004, Taki, Lome, and their newborn baby returned home to Santa Ana for 'Afa's wedding. Lu'isa and I flew to the US to attend this happy occasion. I was able to have a heart-to-heart talk with Taki. I explained to him the challenge I was facing in Tonga as the ferry business was growing rapidly and his brother Edward ('Etu) was working as the engineer, but I needed a trustworthy electrician. I asked Taki to consider moving to Tonga and using his field of expertise to help grow and strengthen our family business.

As expected, Taki asked for some time to think over this proposal, and I thanked him for the consideration. About a month and a half later, I received a call from Taki saying, "Dad, I have thought carefully about your proposal, and I accept without reservation." I was thrilled and thanked my son sincerely. On January 12th, 2005, Taki and Lome landed at the Fua'amotu Airport, which was a huge blessing. Thinking about his innocent-like character, his pure heart, being obedient without question, and his total faith in my role as the patriarch of our family, these were some of my son's qualities I shall never forget. The sum of many precious memories of him brings tears of pure joy, and I thank the Lord for blessing me with such a wonderful son.

Taki and his family, Lome, Walter & Mona

In November of 2005, Taki and his family flew back to California as Lome was pregnant with their second child. Monalisa Maka-ko-Fele'unga Uata was born on December 9th, 2005, and then they all returned to Tonga in early 2006. I assigned Taki to work in the oil tanker *Punalei* as the electrician, and he was proficient and good at this job. Soon he proved his capability a nd he was honest in his dealings, reliable, and trustworthy. He gained the workers' respect even at such a young age. I granted more authority to him to run the operations and reminded him that with authority comes great responsibility, and he replied, "I'm keenly aware, Dad, of its weight."

Taki's responsibility on the boat kept him away from his young family for weeks, leaving his wife and two children at home with his mother and me. Sometimes, it would be months that he was gone when the boat traveled to Fiji for fuel refilling. Taki made an accurate account of the money collected from the boat and turned it over as soon as they docked in Tongatapu. Salome often complained to him about the time they spent apart, but Taki, in his gentle way, always calmed her down as he carried on the responsibility I assigned him. It had been years, and Taki, being a faithful son, still abided by every request I made of him and showed no resistance.

Taki and his family, Lome, Walter & Mona

I still remember the echo of Taki's voice repeatedly saying, "Mom and Dad, I have told my wife that we will be the ones taking care of you both when you grow older, and we will tell our kids when they are old enough to understand." At this time, both his mother and I brushed it off because we still felt strong and couldn't imagine being taken care of. Nonetheless, Taki was persistent with his wish, and with every family meeting we had, he reiterated this message. Everything his mother and I told him to do, he executed it exactly as he was asked. I never heard any murmuring fall from his lips, only, "Yes, Mom. Yes, Dad." Taki is every parent's dream of a golden child.

The call I received from Ha'apai on the 24th of June 2010 was my breaking point. I listened through the telephone receiver

Lu'isa & 'Uliti in mourning

Lome, Toa & Peta mourning over Taki's body

unable to respond as I was informed of my son's passing; it brought me to my knees as they buckled over this harrowing news. There was no time to think rationally because all I wanted to do was to see for myself and confirm his identity. We left that same evening from Tongatapu to Ha'apai to bring my son's body back home.

As we arrived and the details surrounding his death unfolded, it was devastating and heroic at the same time. A worker, who was also Taki's friend, named Ula Manuofetoa, was working down at the engine deck of the MV *Punalei* cleaning out some

Tu'i, 'Afa, Lu'isa & 'Uliti crying on the side looking at Taki's coffin

'Uliti, Melelupe & Naite Lahi crying looking over Taki's coffin

Lu'isa crying over Taki's body

empty tankers. Another worker alerted Taki, who was nearby, that Ula had not come back up for a while and there might be a possibility of gas leakage. Taki flew over in a flash to check it out. Eyewitness account of coworkers saw Taki leap over the top deck to help his friend without thinking about his own safety or to take proper precautions. Taki charged down the stairs, grabbed Ula, and as he started to drag Ula's body up the stairway, the gas fumes occupied his lungs, and with lack of oxygen, Taki took his last breath and died with his friend on his back.

Breaking Point

Naite Lahi & Toa crying over Taki's coffin

Lavi, Lu'isa & 'Uliti mourning silently to the side of Taki's coffin

Naite Lahi, Toa, 'Ofa, Matapule, 'Uliti & Lu'isa in a prayer offering by family and loved ones

Overcome with grief, I cried, "Oh Lord, why?" as I poured out my sorrow in desperation. This was the darkest moment of my adult life. I had lost all logic and reasoning, except to mourn an avalanche of tears as in that moment my spirit was engulfed in despair. Writing about this tragic event that I buried deep in my heart for years is like cutting open a wound that has not healed. Yet it felt so free and therapeutic in a way as my spirit slowly regained serenity, peace, and acceptance in the process.

To this day, Taki's wife and children have stayed true to his wish as they are currently my caretakers since I had my stroke in 2012. Each day when I see their faces, it reminds me of my obedient son. When Salome is questioned as to why she is still taking care of me, she replies simply, "Because, with every breath he had in this life, Taki's only wish was to make sure his parents are taken care of. So, I will carry that responsibility to make his wish come true."

Even his two children, Walter and Mona, are by our sides, serving their grandmother and me diligently and lovingly. Some days I can see the longing in their eyes as they miss their dad, and I pull them close and whisper that I miss him too. We unanimously

'Uliti lifting up Walter to kiss his father good-bye

Lome holding Monalisa to say her final good-bye to her father

'Uliti holding Walter & Lome looking over Taki's body

nod our heads and smile as we reflect on his precious memory as a father, a husband, a brother, a friend, a colleague, and a son.

I would be amiss if I didn't write a letter to my son in honor of his memory. May it reach him even in spirit.

> To My Beloved Son Takilesi,
>
> Where do I begin to express my outcry, for you left without a word, not even to say good-bye, for reasons I cannot understand and only God knows why?
>
> You came as a tiny miracle, a four-pounder extraordinaire, a fighter since birth bringing joy beyond compare, then broke my heart in pieces as you left me standing there.
>
> Takilesi, of all the worldly treasures, diamonds, silver, or gold; of all the precious gifts in life, however great or small; to have you as my son was the greatest gift of all.
>
> All alone in my sorrow, I let out an anguished cry, how can heaven be so cruel and take away my joy and pride?; drowned in my distress and emotions so raw, I accepted defeat with my head bowed to the floor.
>
> So many unsaid words, I wish I could express; so many regrets and bygones, I wish I could erase; so many moments I've missed out, I wish I could regain; but now that you are gone, time has robbed me of this chance.
>
> If only you can hear me, son, calling out your name; Douglas 'Ofa-ki-Ha'angana Uata, you are not only my beloved son but also my dearest friend; you are my hero indeed, and I am your greatest fan; may your soul rest in peace, until we meet again.
>
> With all my love,
>
> Dad.

Chapter 20

Discovered Treasure

The Power of Your Mind

What is the secret to your success? Many have asked this simple yet thought-provoking question. Even I am amazed as I try to figure out how I overcame most challenges life had dealt me. As I was writing my story, I asked myself repeatedly, the why question. Just when I think I know the answer, another "Why?" is asked as my own life is ever-changing as it continues to unfold.

I will embark on figuring out these questions as I continue to grow and evolve on my earthly journey, revealing the mysteries of the infinite as my mind is enlightened.

First and foremost, I know like I know like I know, that I am a son of a Heavenly Father. With this assurance of faith embedded in my resolve, it sparked an aura of nobility as I envisioned God's fingerprints all over my DNA. But how can that be, given my birth circumstances and humble upbringing?

I found great comfort as I related to what God affirmed to Jeremiah, "Before I formed thee in the belly I knew thee, and before thou camest forth out of the womb I sanctified thee, and I ordained thee a prophet unto the nations." (Jeremiah king james version, chapter1, verse5, 2001)[69] These words ring with power as though God was speaking directly to me. I replaced Jeremiah's name with my own, and like a heavenly decree, this affirmation entered my mind: "'Uliti, doubt not your divine purpose for I am your Creator and before you were born, I knew you. Fear not, for I am within you."

Armed with this conviction, I pondered and reflected as I quieted my mind to tune out the noise and allow the essence of my spirit to emerge. Like lessons I learned from Sunday School, "to be in the world but not of the world." I was born with a noble birthright in this body to have a human experience. I do not have to succumb to its influences but rise above the world's limitations and realize my God-given potential.

As far back as I can remember, I had been asked hundreds of times over how I rose from poverty to prosperity and how I created wealth out of nothing. Truth be told, my answers were general, vague, and incoherent due to my lack of comprehension. Even my children and grandchildren asked me to teach them how I did it, as though it was a highly guarded secret. I found myself unable to articulate a thorough answer because in order for me to teach them the concept, I must have a clear understanding of the process. I attributed my success to hard work and being frugal. But many have countered my claim, saying that the result of them working their fingers to the bone was nothing more than mediocre living. So, I added luck and sacrifice, dedication, and commitment; but all of this advice was lacking and offered no real direction. What could it be then, I asked myself? I grew in frustration and wanted the dark clouds of confusion to lift and clarity to set in.

I turned inward for self-reflection as I combed through events of my life experiences. Everything pointed to the day my father passed away. I was keenly aware of the circumstances we were thrown into given the unexpected passing of my father. The sound of Mother's cry still rings in my ear like thunder. The sad and hopeless look in her eyes is still vivid in my memory like yesterday. The firmness of her voice as she shared her hope and aspiration to me at the tender age of four was written in my heart and buried deep into my subconscious mind. I was transformed, almost like an out-of-body experience where I made the decision that failure was not an option. "I must, and I will be the provider for our family."

Through self-assessment, this discovered treasure hidden in plain sight that I was unaware existed was the power of my subconscious mind. Although I tapped into this dimension out of desperation for survival, nonetheless, I felt as though something had been disturbed and awakened within me. I had an epiphany of consciousness as I traced everything back to a singular moment in time.

All the bells and whistles went off in my head like a symphony of fireworks exploding, and a recurring decision came to light. Whatever challenges I faced, whatever difficulty I encountered, whatever situation I was put in, whatever life threw at me, even the impossible, I already made up my mind that failure was not an option. Now the dots began to connect, and I was finally able to formulate my thought process to understand this newfound breakthrough concept, "Whatever a man thinketh, he will become," as in the Bible, "For as he thinketh in his heart, so is he…" (Proverbs king james version, chapter23, verse7, 2001)[70]

This is it. This is the discovered treasure. There is no outside force greater than the power within. I attribute my success to this newfound realization as I tapped into the unlimited power of my subconscious mind. Just below the threshold of consciousness lies the subconscious dimension. You don't need to seek it; you already have it within you. The infinite intelligence of your subconscious mind will reveal to you everything you need to know. Though invisible, its forces are mighty. The law of your subconscious mind is the law of belief, which means what you think about, will come about. Your subconscious mind is the treasure house within you.

    This is how I was able to escape the harsh reality of my life, by tapping into the power of my subconscious mind, and within this realm, I allowed my imagination to take over and create the life I saw in my mind. Although the reality of my childhood dictated otherwise and the hardship of life was real and cruel, my subconscious mind was my escape. At the end of the day, when I lay down, scared, and alone, I said a silent prayer and asked God for protection for Mother, Venisi, and me. Then my mind took off like a rocket as my imagination began to create, almost like a parallel universe. Even in my young mind, I already lived in this new world constructed with my imagination, and with these thoughts, I fell asleep.

    As soon as daybreak arrived, I was back into my current reality, but each night, I escaped in my thoughts, and with each dream and vision, my belief grew stronger. It was like a tug-of-war between my reality and my imaginative mind, and it seemed as though I took three steps forward then four steps back. My two worlds, reality and the imaginary, collided. At an incredibly young age, I learned to discipline my mind because that was the only thing I had total control of. As I grew older, I lived an extremely strict and disciplined lifestyle. From the time I woke up to the time I went to sleep, everything was planned and executed accordingly, from meal breaks to even everyday mundane personal grooming.

    In my youth, I began a new ritual, adding to my nightly routine. I lay outside on the open grass looking up and wondered, what intelligence created this mesmerizing brightness of the stars and the crescent shape of the moon? Captivated by this sight, I took my hand and made a circle around my eyes to focus on the magnificent beauty of the dark sky with glimmering lights. I continued this daily ritual throughout my adolescent years, and it helped me to escape and dream.

Year after year, nothing had manifested or came remotely close to resembling the world I had dreamed up in my imagination, but regardless, I was stern and undeterred in the possibilities. I pressed forward more diligently with unwavering determination filtering out negative thoughts and replacing them with positive words of affirmation. But most importantly, I did not allow my environment, family, circle of friends, surroundings, or current circumstances to influence my mind. I constantly told myself that the reality I was living was an illusion, and my belief of a better world was the driving force. I imagined a life of abundance, and I experienced the joy of living to see this wish fulfilled.

When I got married and started a family, these nightly rituals I had practiced for years started to take shape, and my memory took me back to what I felt that night at the beach looking out into the ocean. I began a new ritual of waking up early in the morning when it was still dark outside, and after I said my prayer, I ran to the wharf and stood there with my arms stretched as I embraced the ocean breeze and the saltiness of its mist as my imagination took over. On many occasions, I lost track of time, and I was completely engulfed by the images I saw of boats rushing across the waters.

I never shared my imagination with anyone, not even my wife, Lu'isa, because I was the only one who believed in what I saw. If I told another soul, I would be ridiculed as a dreamer and be told to return to my senses, so I dared not share my thoughts. As each day began religiously with these daily rituals, my mind expanded as well as my imagination. Still, my reality was nothing but the opposite of what I imagined, but nothing convinced me to give up.

My daily practice turned into habits, my habits turned into beliefs, and my beliefs turned into reality. Slowly but surely, things began to shift as I followed the instincts of my thoughts. Whatever opportunity opened, I grabbed it. Wherever my thoughts led me, I followed. Some people called it luck, but I saw it as preparation meeting opportunity. Understanding the laws of the universe, I sent out the energy of my thoughts, and I attracted the same frequency of energy and entered into this intangible force. I was no longer the observer as I became distinctly aware of my conscious thoughts. I was now a creator of endless possibilities through the infinite power of my subconscious mind, and I created the reality I envisioned with my imagination.

My family started to grow and with each birth of a child came more responsibilities. I began to intensify my daily rituals and heightened my awareness of higher power, which manifested through my prayers. I felt the essence of my spirit with great emotions when I uttered words of gratitude to my Heavenly Father. I started to include my children in my morning rituals as I drove with them in the car every morning to the wharf so I could meditate. My vision became clearer. I literally saw boats on the water, and I added colors to them during this dreamlike stage to give them more life. I harnessed all of the positive energy of gratitude and happiness I felt, then released it out to the universe as though it had already happened.

It was like my world had transformed and everything I saw in my imagination had slowly manifested and turned into a new reality. It was as though my thoughts became a well-oiled engine, repeatedly proving that whatever I saw in my mind became real. And if that wasn't enough, I saw that I was attracting more abundance everywhere I turned, and everything I touched became profitable. I was living in the world that I created with the figment of my imagination when I was younger.

There were things that I was sure of. If you want to change your reality, your circumstance, your world, and live the life of your dreams, you cannot look for any outside force because the power is already within you. If you continue to look through the lenses of your familiar past, it will become your predictable future. As the famous Albert Einstein once said, "Insanity is doing the same thing over and over again and expecting different results." (Albert Einstein, 2021)[71]

Take risks and be adventurous. Climb the tallest tree and have a bird's eye view of your life. If you don't like what you see, change it. If what you want seems unreasonable, difficult, or downright impossible, create it. Don't wait for something or someone to hand over your dream life. Go get it and make no apologies for it and be the change you imagine.

If you dwell in self-pity thinking, poor me; if you feel hatred toward someone because he/she did something hurtful to you; if you are jealous because of…; if you cannot forgive someone because you were a victim of…; these are all negative emotions, and you will only attract more negative experiences into your life. You cannot feed your mind negative thoughts and expect a positive outcome. The Bible tells us, "…for whatsoever a man soweth, that shall he also reap." (Galatians king james version, chapter6, verse7, 2001)[72] If you plant an apple seed, do not expect to get an orange. It is the same principle with our minds. If we feed our minds with good thoughts, we will produce good emotions, and we will find ourselves happy and enjoy life.

Our mind has unlimited power, and only through meditation and practice will you be able to tap into that power. Shift your focus to the now and be present. This is all you've got, right here, right now, at this very moment. Because once this moment is gone, you can never get it back. We all have twenty-four hours available for us each day to use at our disposal, but it is how we choose to use it that differentiates success from failure. Once this day is gone, once this moment passes, you can never get it back. Time cannot be bought, delayed, or borrowed. When you have it, use it wisely or it will fly away and disappear.

Utilize the time that you have to create the future you want, even if your current reality feels otherwise. Fight off the urge to conform and tell your mind that you are the master and it is the servant, so it must serve your wish and desire. Then command your mind to make your dream come true, and it must obey. This is my life's lesson and my experiences that I leave behind as a legacy for future generations of my family to know that you have unlimited power and potential. You are a child of God and you were born with a noble birthright and endowed with the intelligence of the Creator.

Chapter 21

Acres of Diamonds

Look Within—Happiness is an Inside Job

What wisdom can I leave behind for future generations? Which significant part of my journey can I impart of my life experiences that will be most impactful? What is my takeaway from living a blissful life, boundless and abundant? The scriptures tell us, "…men are that they might have joy" (Book of Mormon, chapter2, 2001)73; and if this is the purpose of our birth, to live in a joyful state of being during our earthly journey, then how do we demystify this abstract concept?

As with everything in life, a person's interpretation is based on his/her perception as it is influenced by past experiences. The responsibility of the mind is to ensure our survival. From the very mundane daily routines to the complexity of the body's functions. Our brain keeps a meticulous record of every moment and takes snapshots of events accompanied by strong emotions. Having said this, I will unravel my understanding of this mystic abstract notion, imparting a legacy of wisdom gained through my own life experiences.

I cannot say with certainty how many times I've heard these phrases: If only I was rich…if only I was born under different circumstances…if only I weighed fifty pounds lighter…if only I had a beautiful face…if only I had the perfect relationship…if only I could find love…if only I lived in a mansion…if only I was lucky enough to be born into a wealthy family…then I would be happy. I won't lie; I wished things would have been different when I grew up, but my attitude was due to ignorance. As I evolved and took control of my mind, looking back in hindsight, I would not have traded anything in my past because it got me to where I am today.

So many people spend a lifetime looking outside of themselves for something or someone to make them happy, and it is a fantasy and wishful thinking. Say, for example, I had wished to get a new car. The circuitry of the brain fires up and makes you excited, therefore creating an elevated emotion of happiness. But soon after you take possession of the vehicle, the happy feelings subside, and you then search for something else to feel happy again. The illusion that material things can make you happy or you need someone to make you feel loved is nothing but a whirlpool of fallacy.

One such twisted idea accepted by many is that money is the root of all evil. When, in fact, it is the love of money that churns the seed of greed, which branches out to breed lies, theft, selfishness, hatred, comparison, deceit, envy, jealousy, abuse of power, etc….You will always end up wanting more, as though nothing can ever satisfy your desires. To combat such a mindset, the word of God tells us these poignant truths: "…the fruit of the Spirit is love, joy, peace, longsuffering, gentleness, goodness, faith." (Galatians king james version, chapter5, verse7, 2001)[74] Through experiences, I have learned that being content, feeling satisfied, and feeling fulfilled induced an emotion of happiness. If one does not experience this feeling of joy, then he/she will be on an endless search for something or someone to fill that void.

I read this inspirational story that puts this concept into perspective and demonstrates the analogy of which I speak. Back in 1869, Russell Conwell wrote his famous essay "Acres of Diamonds," based on something he heard from a tour guide as he was traveling in the Middle East and going down the Tigris and Euphrates rivers.

> There once lived not far from the River Indus an ancient Persian by the name of Ali Hafed and he owned a very large farm; with orchards, grain-fields, and gardens; and was a wealthy and contented man. One day an ancient Buddhist priest, one of the wise men of the East, visited.
>
> He spoke of "Diamond as a congealed drop of sunlight."
>
> The old priest told Ali Hafed that if he had one diamond the size of his thumb, he could purchase the county, and if he had a mine of diamonds, he could place his children upon thrones through the influence of their great wealth. Ali Hafed heard all about diamonds, how much they were worth, and a poor man went to his bed that night. He had not lost anything, but he was poor because he was discontented and discontented because he feared he was poor.
>
> Early in the morning, he sought out the priest…
>
> Said Ali Hafed, "I will go."
>
> He sold his farm, collected his money, left his family in charge of a neighbor, and away he went in search

of diamonds. He began his search at the Mountains of the Moon. Afterward, he came around into Palestine, then wandered on into Europe, and at last when his money was all spent. He was in rags, wretchedness, and poverty, he stood on the shore of that bay at Barcelona, in Spain, when a great tidal wave came rolling in between the pillars of Hercules, and the poor, afflicted, suffering, dying man could not resist the awful temptation to cast himself into that incoming tide. He sank beneath its foaming crest, never to rise in this life again.

The man who purchased Ali Hafed's farm one day led his camel into the garden to drink, and as that camel put its nose into the shallow water of that garden brook, Ali Hafed's successor noticed a curious flash of light from the white sands of the stream. He pulled out a black stone having an eye of light reflecting all the hues of the rainbow. He took the pebble into the house and put it on the mantel that covers the central fires and forgot all about it.

A few days later this same old priest came in to visit Ali Hafed's successor, and the moment he opened that drawing-room door, he saw that flash of light on the mantel, and he rushed up to it and shouted:

"Here is a diamond! Has Ali Hafed returned?"

"Oh no, Ali Hafed has not returned, and that is not a diamond. That is nothing but a stone we found right out here in our garden."

"But," said the priest, "I tell you I know a diamond when I see it. I know positively that is a diamond."

Then, together, they rushed out into that old garden and stirred up the white sands with their fingers, and lo! There came up other more beautiful and valuable gems than the first. "Thus," said the guide to me, "was discovered the diamond mine of Golconda, the most magnificent diamond mine in all the history of mankind…the largest on earth came from that mine."

The old Arab guide said, "Had Ali Hafed remained at home and dug in his cellar, or underneath his wheat fields or in his garden, instead of wretchedness, starvation, and death by suicide in a strange land, he would have had 'acres of diamonds.' For every acre of that old farm, yes, every shovelful, afterward revealed gems which since have decorated the crowns of monarchs." (Russell Conwel, 2019)[75]

My takeaway is the same as the moral of this story. Had Ali Hafed stayed home and dug in his backyard, he would have discovered that he lived on acres of diamonds and be rich beyond his wildest dreams. But because he was discontent and went looking for diamonds elsewhere to fill his desires, thinking there was something more valuable than what he already possessed, he lost his family and died a poor, lonely man in despair.

Can we identify with or relate to Ali Hafed's story? So many people go out into the world searching aimlessly for material possessions because they are not satisfied with what they already have and fail to recognize that we each stand in our own acres of diamonds. Whether you live in a mansion or a humble dwelling, you do not need to look far and wide because all the wealth in the world will not bring you happiness. Look within your own backyard and see your family as a treasure. Dig up your gift. Search deep within to find it because it was given only to you, so figure it out and live up to your potential that God gifted you with.

When the feeling of content sets in, you will be happy even when lacking, but if you are not content, you won't be happy even when plentiful. In the words of Rabbi Meir Leibush (Malbim), "A joyful heart makes a cheerful face; A sad heart makes a despondent mood: All the days of a poor person are wretched, but contentment is a feast without end." (Contentment, 2021)[76] In Shakespeare's *Henry VIII*, Act III, it reads: "Tis better to be lowly born, And range with humble livers in content, Than to be perk'd up in a glistering grief, And wear a golden sorrow." (Henry VIII (play), 2021)[77] Benjamin Franklin put it well: "Contentment makes poor men rich; discontent makes rich men poor."

We live in a materialistic world, and we have been taught that the more you get, the richer you will be and the happier you will become. We think, "I'll be happy when I get married," and a whole array of similar thought processes because we have been brainwashed to think that "the grass is always greener on the other side of the fence." We often wish to have what others have and never think much about what we already have. Contentment is being satisfied with what you have and with who you are—right now at this very moment. Regardless of your current situation, whether you're rich or poor, heavy or slender, smart or uneducated, a business owner or unemployed, married or single, our circumstance has no bearing on how we choose to feel.

In his letter to the church in Philippi, the Apostle Paul shares the secret to being content:

> Not that I speak in respect of want: for I have learned, in whatsoever state I am, therewith to be content.
>
> I know both how to be abased, and I know how to abound: every where and in all things I am instructed both to be full and to be hungry, both to abound and to suffer need.
>
> I can do all things through Christ which strengthened me. (Philippians king james version, chapter4, verses 11-13, 2009)[78]

Paul told Timothy that "...But godliness with contentment is great gain. For we brought nothing into this world, and it is certain we can carry nothing out. And having food and raiment let us be therewith content. But they that will be rich fall into temptation and a snare, and into many foolish and hurtful lusts, which drown men in destruction and perdition.." (1 Timothy king james version, chapter6, verses 6-9, 2001)[79]

Life is complex and ever-changing. Some days we feel empowered and productive, and other days, we feel defeated and drained. We will experience situations that are uplifting and inspiring, and others will be challenging and draining. We will experience ups and downs, triumphs and defeats, good times and bad. Sometimes, it is smooth sailing, and everything flows and feels easy, and other times, we feel overwhelmed, and life becomes a real struggle. But when we live in a state of contentment, we're happy regardless, and we're able to navigate through the complexity of life.

Everyone desperately searches for happiness. The question is, how? How can we be happy? For many people, the answer is to have more—more money, more fame, more achievements, and more stuff. I don't think that is the right answer, though. Why? Because wanting more is a never-ending loop, like a Catch-22. Yes, you might be happy for a short period when you get what you want, but then after a while, you want or need even more to be happy because you're trying to fill your life with material things, and it is not sustainable.

The wisdom gained through my own experience made me want to understand a deeper meaning of happiness and being content. What does contentment truly mean if money can't buy it and poverty doesn't provide it? Contrary to popular belief, it is not simply being satisfied with what you have or where you are, but in addition to this, it is knowing God's plan for your life, having the conviction to live it, and believing that God's peace is greater than the world's problems.

In moments of chaos and confusion, I immersed myself in meditation, allowing my mind to be clear and be centered as I tuned out the noise and rose to higher conscious awareness. In this heightened state of being, God's words resonated and penetrated my soul to its core with this passage:

> Lay not up for yourselves treasures upon earth, where moth and rust doth corrupt, and where thieves break through and steal:

> But lay up for yourselves treasures in heaven, where neither moth nor rust doth corrupt, and where thieves do not break through nor steal:
>
> For where your treasure is, there will your heart be also. (evangelist s. m., matthew king james version, chapter6, verses19-21, 2001)[80]

The transparency of the words impressed upon my mind in a moment of contemplation opened my awareness to appreciate treasures of eternal value such as family, friends, and people that we love because they are the ones that make our lives meaningful and give purpose to our existence. They share our joy and sorrow with us, provide comfort in times of need, fill the void with love and acceptance, and are our biggest cheerleaders. The circle of family, close or extended, the community of neighbors, our friends, and our peers are an extension of ourselves because they play a vital role in shaping our perspective and experiences in life. They are true treasures that won't rust or decay and will even withstand the duration of space and time.

Contentment has deepened my understanding of God's grace. Have you considered asking the Lord what He wants you to learn in your present circumstance instead of telling God what you want Him to change? As we look inward and do some soul searching, we begin to understand that happiness is an inside job. Take a walk in the woods and admire the flowers blooming, smell the roses and the magnolia, the wisteria, and the freesia, and allow their alluring fragrance to induce an appreciation for the power of creation.

Take a walk on the beach, breathe in the ocean breeze, and marvel at the beautiful colors of the sun rising or setting. And if these options are not available, just step out to your backyard, look around and admire nature and breathe in the fresh air. Read a good book, lose yourself in your imagination, create the life you want, and feel the joy of a fulfilled wish. Indulge in your enlightened journey and learn new concepts with continued education. Listen to inspiring music, close your eyes, and allow its melody to sink in and be absorbed by the lyrics in their poetic arrangement. By being aware and being present, these simple moments will uplift your spirit and elevate your emotions to a deeper understanding of life.

When you reach this level of consciousness, you are content. You smile for no reason because you feel happy, you see beauty all around you, you feel compassion for others, you are moved to act as your heart dictates. Nothing in your outside world has changed, yet you live in this state of joy because of who you are on the inside. Happiness is not a destination for you to reach; it is simply a state of being and one that you choose.

Chapter 22

Mausoleum

Buried but Not Forgotten

Sir Isaac Newton, speaking of the contributions of his predecessors, said, "If I have seen further than others, it is because I've stood on the shoulders of giants." (Isaac Newton, 2021)[81] The wisdom in this statement is in the humble acknowledgment of the contributions by those who have gone before us and paved the way so that we may stand on their shoulders to see further and do better. Such was true in my case with the two iconic people who had been constants in my journey through thick and thin, peaks and valleys, joyous and sad moments of life: Mother and Venisi.

We were a synchronized trio in heart, mind, and spirit. Nothing could penetrate our sacred circle because all we had was each other as we faced life's challenges and overcame them together. We were an unbreakable team of like-mindedness and unanimously agreed with each other in basically everything. Whether the issue was big or small, or the task was difficult or easy, or the consequences and risks were equally epic, whatever it was, we stood united in our decisions. Although we were few in number, we were a force to be reckoned with, simply because we had each other's back.

After eighty-plus years of life's journey, I look back to the day Mother and Venisi agreed that it was my role to provide for the family. It was as though their decision was planned by divine design as it is not normal for a younger brother/son to be given such responsibilities, which are usually reserved for the oldest. I can clearly see now that the two of them were in harmony with the spirit of our Creator and Savior. From the moment at the beach when we collectively concurred that I would be the provider of the family, an unspoken unified alliance formed the beginning of how we modeled our family, one for all and all for one.

This was a potent act of love that shifted our focus momentarily from reality to the power and energy that surged through us. Thus, my brother freely agreed and willingly sacrificed his schooling to work so that I could receive my education. The sacrifices are now as clear as the eye can see as they were lovingly offered because of His spirit that we felt, which was and has always been the cornerstone of my journey as our family's provider.

The three of us individually had a destined role in our family dynamics. Whether it was spoken or unexpressed, assumed or expected, asked or unwanted, we each played our part beautifully, like a harmonious tune by a well-orchestrated symphony. It was an innate mutual understanding, unspoken yet accepted by all three of us as our familial fate. We saw each other as part of a whole.

Mother was the captain of our ship as she steered and adjusted sails, maneuvering through the turbulent and calm waters of life with a keen eye for opportunities, constantly seeking a better destination for us to land. I was the curious one with a wild and vivid imagination, which enhanced my visionary gift with a non-conforming point of view, an unsurpassed creative talent, and a knack for business, hence, why I was chosen to be the provider. Venisi was the protector with his mature personality. He spoke with confidence and commanded respect, was strong in stature, caring in nature, and was the voice of reason with a deep sense of loyalty. He stood guard as the gatekeeper for our family's safety.

Mother's legal birth name was Sulieti Puafisi, but she was known by her nickname, Melepua, and that's what she was called her entire life. She came from a family of six children with a very humble upbringing, and her parents were Fifita and Siosaia Finau. I've wondered how I could pay tribute to the woman who birthed me as she was larger than life in my young mind. Whatever challenges she faced, whatever difficulties she encountered, whatever pain she felt,

Melepua's family tree, with her parents and siblings

after she let out a good cry, she wiped her face dry, and with conviction in her voice, she would declare, "It is what it is." That was her way of accepting everything life threw at her, and she had to deal with it somehow.

Mother had a feisty attitude and disdain for self-pity. When she saw me wallowing in sadness and moping around with my head cast down, she shook me up and knocked some sense into my head, saying, "'Uliti, stop feeling sorry for yourself. Snap out of it and get a grip." It was her way of reminding me that if life throws you a lemon, don't be bitter about it; make lemonade. Thinking back about Mother's personality, she was a woman of strength—physically, emotionally, and mentally, with good common sense and many

'Uliti combing Melepua's hair

Toa to the right, Melepua in the middle & Venisi to the left

positive attributes. I remember when I didn't want to leave home for school, and I would cry and cry for days on end, not wanting to be separated from her and Venisi. Mother, in a stern voice, told me how it is and did not dilute the truth; then she left me alone to process my thoughts, and she went about her daily chores. Observing her demeanor and watching her carry on despite our circumstances made me rid myself of self-pity and man up to become strong just like her.

When I finally built a home big enough for my family, I moved Mother in to stay with us. She was afraid of electricity, so I built a separate house with indoor plumbing but no electricity for her in the back. She used a kerosene lamp for light at night, and one of my daughters, Melenaite, moved and stayed with Mother to look after her. She had an outside kitchen where she enjoyed doing her cooking.

Every Sabbath day, Mother did the cooking for our whole family. She woke up at the first rooster's crow when it was still dark outside and started prepping for her *umu* (where food is cooked in an underground oven). There was no changing her menu and no substitutes either; it had *manioke paku* (cassava baked until it's burnt, then scrape off the black flakes and it leaves you with a crunchy cassava piece); *lu sipi* (lamb with onion cooked in coconut milk covered with taro leaves); *lo'i lesi* (papaya cooked in coconut milk), and *to'ukutu* (a dessert made of flour, sugar, and coconut flakes mixed with water to form a dough and baked in the coconut shell). The aroma of the fire burning to make charcoal for the underground oven was our Sunday morning alarm clock. We knew we would eat good food and anticipated the feast Mother prepared for us.

Lu'isa on the right, Melenaite Sr in the middle & 'Uliti on the left

Toward the end of Mother's life, she had stomach cancer, and we tried to persuade her to go to New Zealand for medical treatment, but she was so afraid of flying. We begged and begged, and she saw the sadness in our eyes, which changed her mind, and she finally agreed to go.

We flew to New Zealand, and the prognosis was dire as she had reached stage-4 cancer, so we flew back to Tonga to spend the remainder of her days at home together.

September 26th, 1984, Mother passed away quietly in the middle of the night at home. All of us, Lu'isa and I and all our children, were all by Mother's side as she transitioned over on her final journey back home peacefully. It happened around one a.m. and it was a beautiful experience to witness. After a while, we had all left to quickly prepare the big house for the funeral the next morning. Around four a.m. when the preparation was done, the women went back to get Mother's body dressed. Here was my daughter Melenaite right next to Mother's body; having exhausted herself from crying, she fell asleep right next to Mother's body. As my daughter woke up and saw her grandmother, she let out this loud cry as she mourned by her side. Lu'isa and I were watching through the louvers in our bedroom, our daughter wailing and moaning in agony. Her emotions so raw, and the echo of her weeping was the most unnaturally soothing sound to my heart. It comforted me knowing that my children felt such deep love for their grandmother. I seconded the words of Abraham Lincoln when he said, "All that I am, or hope to be, I owe to my angel mother." (Mothers, 2021)[82]

Melepua's headstone

I can honestly say with genuineness and sincerity, Thank you, Mother. I was strong when I was on your shoulders and became a man. You taught me life is hard but manageable, and you showed me to sacrifice and work hard. You sowed the seed of determination in my heart. Even when I was at my wit's end, and it seemed like I couldn't make it through, you told me just to stand, stand tall and stand firm with zeal and conviction. Even through the storm, rain or shine, hurt or pain, just keep standing, and after you have done all that is humanly possible, that's when God begins His work. Such were the loving memories of my angel mother, Melepua.

Venisi, my older brother, was my best friend and my protector as I felt safe under his shadow. We did everything together

Mausoleum

Venisi & 'Uliti

as we were two separate bodies but with one mind. We could finish off each other's sentences, and we were inseparable in heart, mind, and spirit. He was my biggest cheerleader, and he made me feel as though I was the smartest kid in the world. He boosted my confidence by making me believe that I can do anything I put my mind to. If I ever expressed doubt or fear, he would say, "You've got this, little man. I believe in you." How could I disappoint my brother? The thought of disappointing him was unbearable because he had so much faith in my ability, even when I absolutely had none in myself. I often asked him, "Venisi, why do you always say such nice things about me? Are you doing it so I can feel better about myself?"

He answered in such a loving manner, "No, little man. I truly believe you are capable of just about anything because you're smart and creative."

When I asked him to explain his meaning, he replied, "Oh 'Uliti, if only you can see you through my eyes. You are perfect and the smartest boy I know." Talk about pressure. I felt it on every level of my being because I did not want to disappoint my brother.

Although I did not fully comprehend the sacrifice Venisi did for me when I was little, now, when I look back, I am so grateful for his willingness to forgo his schooling and stay behind to help Mother to put me through school. When we both became adults and had our own families, occasionally I would ask, "Venisi, do you have any regrets?" and without hesitation, he said, "Absolutely none. I knew my role was to help you fulfill your divine role of providing for our family." Then I pressed him more and asked, "What if I had failed?"

"Oh, but you wouldn't fail," he replied promptly, "because I saw fire in your eyes and felt the passion in your heart, and that's a recipe for success." When I used to campaign for parliament, Venisi was my biggest supporter. When I would hear him talk about me, he painted a picture of such high esteem, almost like nobility, and I told him to dial it down a bit because even as an adult, I still didn't see myself in the light my brother saw me. But he laughed it off and told me to let him have his moment because he was speaking his truth. Venisi didn't think I could do any wrong. He said, "'Uliti, your name is spelled with success all over it."

Finally, I gave up and just let him be because it brought him so much joy when he talked about his younger brother. I gave Venisi the taxi business and told him to run it to support his family. A couple of times a week, he stopped by my house to say hi, and we really did not talk much. Just seeing each other was enough. Venisi made it a point to pick up each of my children on their birthdays and take them to town for an ice-cream treat. That left a huge impact on my kids because that treat from their uncle made them feel so special.

On one of Venisi's trips to the house, I could sense something was wrong. I told the kids to go outside and not come back until their uncle left. We started talking, and I finally said to Venisi, "I know you came here for a reason, so let's hear it." His eyes cast downward, and his tone lowered as he struggled to say what was on his mind. I interrupted him mid-sentence and told him, "Whatever it is you need, I will help you," but Venisi couldn't bring himself to ask me. I made some phone calls the next day to the bank and figured out the issue. The taxi business was about to go bankrupt, so I paid off the loan and bought him additional cars for his taxi business.

On his next visit, he said, "I don't know what to say to you, 'Uliti, except thank you."

I told him, "There is nothing for you to say, but I have something to say to you, Venisi. 'I've got your back, my brother, just like how you got mine when we were young.'" There was an intense moment of silence where we felt such deep brotherly love toward each other.

Venisi's Tombstone

Venisi, toward the end of his life, got sick and lost his battle with colon cancer on July 5th, 2001. I was absolutely devastated to have lost a fine soul like my brother, for he was kind-hearted and loving without reservations. He was the pinnacle example of compassion with selfless acts of service toward others. He was survived by four of his children, 'Aioema, Holosini, Melepua, and Hiko.

Every Sunday, Venisi's oldest son, Holosini, brought me an *umu* for the Sabbath day in honor of his father as his way of saying, "I remember you, Uncle, through the love my dad had for you." And to this very day, he still does it religiously without fail. Every Sunday at noon, Holosini enters my home with his family to present this meal. I am humbled by the sincerity of his feelings and so touched by his act of kindness as he is a reflection of his father, which creates a loving bond between my nephew and me as our mutual feelings align with our sweet memories of Venisi, a brother and a father.

We all stand on the shoulders of past generations, as depicted in twelfth-century theologian and author John of Salisbury's words, "We are like dwarfs sitting on the shoulders of giants. We see more things that are more distant than they did, not because our sight is superior or because we are taller than they, but because they raise us, and by their great stature, add to ours." (John of Salisbury, 2021)[83] I like to think that when Venisi hoisted me onto his shoulders when I was a kid, that was his way of raising me to realize my dream and fulfill my divine role in our family.

In the early 1990s, I got a plot of land in Tofoa, Tongatapu, and I started to lay the foundation for our new home. The property was not big enough for what I had in mind because I saw our family growing even more now with grandchildren and great-grandchildren on the way. I decided the next best thing was to expand the land out into the waters, so I started the construction project by first laying the foundation for the property by covering the surface with sand, gravel, and rocks to extend the land, then building a fortifying rock wall around the property to protect it from water rising and wind, almost like a dam.

A sunrise photo from our backyard at our home in Tofoa, Tonga Tapu—picture taken in Oct 2021

This was a very long and expensive project. It took truckloads upon truckloads as we proceeded to move where the land ended and water began, which took about eight months. Once the length of the property was to my satisfaction, the construction of the house began. When everything was finished, we moved into our new home in 1993, and we named our property "Maka ko Fele'unga." Many of the children had already moved out and started families of their own, but they know they will always have a home to come back to.

July 10th, 2012, in the early morning hours, I woke up unable to move, and I woke up Lu'isa. I was rushed to Vaiola Hospital, where they declared that I had had a stroke roughly a month before my seventy-sixth birthday. Tonga is not sophisticated enough with medical technology, so I went overseas to America seeking medical treatment. Despite our best efforts, I knew that this illness had gotten the best of me, and I returned to Tonga and accepted the prognosis of my condition.

The stroke paralyzed my legs and my hands and I was wheelchair-bound. The parliament found out my trip was to obtain medical treatment, and it happened while I was serving in my capacity as the minister of health. The parliament reimbursed me for the expenses of my trip and medical costs, and the chair at the time was Lord Fakafanua.

I can hear Mother's voice in my head telling me to accept this fate that life has dealt me and not be bitter about it. My thought process began to shift. Instead of feeling sorry for myself, I started to feel grateful that I am still alive and grateful for my breath. I began to think about mortality and how short life is with each passing day.

The memories of Mother and Venisi and the passing of my two grandsons, George (Tu'i's son) and James Pouanga (Melenaite Sr's son), four years earlier, and my son Takilesi two years prior all came crashing down like an avalanche. I began to feel the cold grounds of my loved ones' burial places at our family plot at Fanga-'o-Pilolevu, and I suddenly felt distant from them. I wanted them closer to me, and I wanted something more secure, a place where they would be sheltered from rain, sun, or wind, and I also wanted a safe haven for my family's final resting place.

George Uata's tombstone

Takilesi Uata's tombstone

James Pouanga Talanoa's tombstone

These ideas consumed my thoughts, so I decided to build a mausoleum right on our property in Tofoa. Once I reached this decision, the project was in full force, and I ordered materials and began the construction of what I envisioned. During the construction, I ordered a family tombstone with all our names imprinted on it, Lu'isa and me, and then we listed all of our eleven children, including when and where they were born. I also ordered a headstone for Mother, Venisi, Takilesi, George, and James.

In 2014, the mausoleum was completed to my satisfaction, and I named it "Uata Cemetery." I had a room for my immediate family and each of our eleven children. I began requesting an official *hikitanga,* where the bodies are allowed to be exhumed and transported to another burial ground. I got the approval, but I wanted to wait until everyone in our family could be in attendance for this sacred procession. The children planned to celebrate my eightieth birthday on August 24th, 2016, and we also planned a Uata Family Reunion. The theme for our reunion was "Return to Your Roots."

Uata Cemetery

All of our children attended as well as our adopted children and many of the grandchildren and great grandchildren.

It was a memorable occasion, and when the day came for us to do the *hikitanga*, the process was carried out with great care, dignity, and honor. All the grandkids stood as a human shield with a big tapa cloth to cover the burial ground area while the work began to exhume the bodies. Men carefully digged open the graves and brought out the coffins. Our daughters and other family elders sat on the ground with oil and poured over the bones as they laid them lovingly in their new coffins and reconstructed the body layout as best as they could.

I sat in my vehicle throughout the duration of this sacred ritual so I can be present and close enough to make sure everything was being handled with utmost care. Upon completion of this procession, the coffins were escorted back to our home, at our property in Tofoa. There we held an intimate family gathering in front of the Uata Cemetery with songs and prayers as we walked down memory lane. It was a moment of celebration, orating their lives and commemorating their place in our hearts, as tears flowed filled with their precious memories. We welcomed our deceased loved ones home then we acknowledged each person by name as they were laid them into their final resting place:

Uata Cemetery

Uata Memorial Plaque

> Melepua Finau Uata~born February 2nd, 1909~died September 26th, 1984
> Venisi Finau Uata~born January 12th, 1934~died July 5th, 2001
> Douglas 'Ofa-ki-Ha'angana Uata~born January 30th, 1977~died June 24th, 2010
> James Pouanga Talanoa~born April 23rd, 1990~died October 31st, 2008
> George Richard Uata~born June 8th, 1990~died October 31st, 2008

Each deceased person had their room for their burial, and there are other rooms for each of our living children to have a final resting place as well. This was a very emotional family gathering as we had children, grandchildren, and great-grandchildren all there paying our respects. I finally felt peace in my heart that I brought my loved ones to their final resting place right at home, *'api Maka-ko-Fele'unga,* so that they know they have not been forgotten.

Overview of the Uata Cemetery

Another Overview of the Uata Cemetery

In closing this chapter, I leave you with one of Maya Angelou's famous quotes: "I come as one, but I stand as ten thousand: I am standing here today, holding the baton for my parents and all my ancestors that have gone before me. They are with me. Watching me, encouraging me to live life to the fullest, do right, be kind, and do well; because in time, it will be my turn to pass on the baton." (Wikipedia, Maya Angelou, 2022)[84]

Chapter 23

Unsung Hero

Lu'isa's Story

Lu'isa Uata

Unsung Hero

One Mother's Day, our late son Takilesi gave Lu'isa a card, and in it, he wrote, "Jesus Christ came to be the Savior of the world; but you mom, you came to be the Savior of our family." The profound depth of his words is the essence of this chapter as it depicts the characteristics of Lu'isa as her story is being shared. Above all else, she is truly a remarkable woman of great faith, unshakable, immovable, undeterred, unwavering, unfaltering, and unyielding in every sense of the divine principle of faith.

Lu'isa's favorite scripture is found in Ether 12:12: "For if there be no faith among the children of men God can do no miracle among them; wherefore, he showed not himself until after their faith." (Book of Mormon, chapter 12, 2019)[85] Every chance Lu'isa gets to talk about faith, her eyes light up as she speaks candidly and enthusiastically about her belief. You can feel the depth of her passion. She can talk for hours on end about faith, telling stories after stories, examples after examples.

Sometimes my children and I will tease her by saying, is there anything else we can talk about, because you say the same thing all the time. And with every ounce of energy, Lu'isa boldly declares, "I shall repeat myself from the rooftop until I see faith embodied by each member of our Uata Family. I want these stories to be handed down for future generations of our family and allow us to continue to walk with faith, in every step of our earthly journey."

Lu'isa was born on Christmas Day, December 25th, 1936, in Feletoa, Vava'u to Mele Lavinia 'Amaka and 'Inoke Tangatafuape Mataele while her parents were serving as missionaries for The Church of Jesus Christ of Latter-Day Saints. She was number five out of six sisters. Her mother passed away due to complications while delivering her last child, in which both mother and child lost their lives. Her father was born handicapped, legally blind, with only one eye working at eighty percent of his vision.

Lu'isa recalled as they moved around from island to island in serving the Lord, she had witnessed her father's faith in action. One such memory she recalled was when they were serving on the islands of Ha'apai. They had no boat to take them when they needed to relocate to a different island. So, her father, 'Inoke, waited until it was low tide, then he would hoist one child at a time over his shoulder and walk across the *'ahanga* (the coral pathway in receding tide) to the other island, drop off one child, then return to get another. Lu'isa recalled this memory with deep emotions as she remembered seeing her father's feet bleeding from the sharpness of the coral rocks, but his faith waxed strong.

During one of these crossings between islands, Lu'isa was waiting for her father to return to take her across the reefs. There were some people fishing with baskets full of fish. She grabbed one small fish, and she tried to bite off its head, but instead, the fish went through to her throat, and she choked, trying to breathe. Her father, 'Inoke, arrived and laid his hands upon her head and gave her a Priesthood blessing, then he used his finger to reach down her throat and pulled out the fish, allowing her to breathe. Lu'isa said that this helped build her faith as she saw how calm her father was, and by laying his hands upon her head, she felt a sense of calmness as well.

Lu'isa recalled another unforgettable memory when they had no food to eat for days. 'Inoke told them to go and get some breadfruit (*mei*), but all that was available was very young and just barely formed fruit. At this stage of the breadfruit, it is considered inedible because of its tartness and bitterness, and its texture is like that of rubber. After he cooked the breadfruit, she remembered how they ate it, almost gagging due to its bitterness. Her father spoke with a firm voice and promised, "Let us eat this food with thanksgiving in our hearts for the Lord is aware of our circumstances, and I promise you, it will be sweet to the taste." Lu'isa recalled after hearing her father say these words, her perspective changed, and her next bite of the young breadfruit did have a sweet taste and it was a miracle that strengthen her faith.

After this incident, her siblings began to murmur about the hardship they had to endure, and in one of their family home evenings, her father made a promise as the patriarch of their family and said, "As we continue to have faith, our family will reach the promised land, the land of milk and honey." Mind you, he said these words back around 1944, and they all wondered how it was going to be possible considering they did not even have enough food to eat.

Lu'isa continued, "I'm not sure about my sisters, but for me, I believed every word my father said." And so, the foundation of her faith had been laid since she was a young girl.

Lu'isa's mother passed away when she just barely turned five years old, and she remembered hearing people's whispers saying, "How is 'Inoke going to take care of these kids?" This gossiping broke her heart, and she was determined to prove them wrong. Around the house, she performed many household chores like cooking, which she had a passion for, cleaning, and washing clothes.

When she turned eight years old, she woke up in the wee hours of the morning, and she turned her cooking passion into a livelihood. She started to make *keke 'isite* (a Tongan cake made from flour, sugar, water, and yeast). After the dough is formed and allowed to rise, you take a handful in your hand and form it into a round ball, then drop it into the hot oil, and when it's cooked, you have a delicious fried dough treat. She did this in the morning before she even went to school; then her father took the keke and sold them.

This money helped supplement their family's income. When Lu'isa returned home from school, she ran over to their plantation field (*'uta*) to help her father weed bushes and clear the field, then brought some food home for them to eat. When they got home, she cooked their meal then cleaned up. It was as though she was replacing their mother. Her sisters were older than her and in their teens, and they also helped, but somehow Lu'isa took on the role of being a mother for the rest of her sisters. As she grew older, she started to help her father cut the coconuts and peel off their flesh, then dry them so they could be sold to get extra money, which helped pay for their schooling.

Lu'isa was strong physically, mentally, and spiritually from a very young age. The loss of her mother taught her to rely on her Savior throughout her childhood. When Lu'isa became a young woman, she entered Liahona for school, but her father didn't have enough money to pay for her schooling. She asked to help out in the cafeteria, where she started working part-time and would get a free meal. It wasn't long before they recognized her talent for cooking, and Lu'isa was made the head cook at Liahona, which helped pay for her school tuition until she graduated from Liahona High School in 1959. With a blind father and no brothers to rely on, poverty taught her the value of hard work and resourcefulness to help support her family.

Lu'isa embraced the next chapter in her life and began looking to start her own family. Her innermost desire led her to communion daily in prayers, pleading with the Lord for an eternal companion to escape poverty. Once a week, every Monday, Lu'isa would fast for twenty-four hours as she prepared her soul before she prayed to God and asked Him to help her attract a man that the Lord saw fit to take her out of poverty.

Once a week Lu'isa fasted faithfully without fail. Against all logic, the Lord's answer was a man even poorer than her, 'Uliti Uata from Ha'ano, Ha'apai. Lu'isa's family was against our marriage, a man from Ha'apai with no land to provide her a place to live. They asked her if she had lost her marbles that she couldn't even see logically. They told her if she decided to marry me, we would live in the bayou since I had no land. But Lu'isa answered, "Even if I have to live with 'Uliti in the bayou, I will make that place a piece of heaven."

Lu'isa relied on her faith as she knew in her heart that I was led to her by the Lord. She was defiant as her family were against our marriage, lashed out at them and said, "If 'Uliti is the answer to my prayer, who am I to question God's will?" and she quoted Psalm 37:4: "Delight thyself also in the Lord: and he shall give thee the desires of thine heart." (Psalms king james version, chapter37, verse 4, 2001)[86] With a heart full of faith, she trusted the Lord and never wavered in her decision to marry me.

From the beginning of our marriage and throughout the early years of our lives together, I questioned what my wife saw in me because I had no faith in my ability to provide, let alone for our new family. But Lu'isa, through sheer determination, did not waver and allowed her faith to prevail through and through. I saw fire in Lu'isa's eyes as she refused to allow hardships to dictate our family's life. The impact of her courage fused with gratitude gave her the ability to rise above a poverty mindset and focus her energy on our daily survival.

Throughout our marriage, we had our ups and our downs, good and bad days, happy and sad moments, tears, and sorrows, but through it all, we managed to stay the course. Our marriage was saved by the grace of her forgiveness, faith, and her love. Whatever I did wrong, Lu'isa forgave me wholeheartedly even when I wondered how she could ever forgive me. When I inquired, Lu'isa answered, "Forgiveness heals the heart, and my choice to forgive is not for you but for myself. Because if I don't forgive, bitterness, anger, and resentment will eat me up inside, so I don't want to live like that."

Lu'isa's faith carried so much truth and power as she endured so many trials and tribulations. Her kind and loving words remain, "Forgiveness is good for the soul." She was able to forgive because of her faith, which sustained her throughout her life. Whether the issue was big or small, significant or not, she took everything before the Lord and prayed for answers. Through her prayers, she would receive promptings and inspiration; then she would act on it. Lu'isa often quoted, "Faith without works is dead," so when we are truly obedient through faith, then we must act accordingly. The Lord will help us, but we must do our part in the equation. We cannot just pray then do nothing. We pray to receive inspiration and answers that we seek, so it is up to us to act upon those promptings and answers.

Lu'isa's perspective on life is filled with pure intention and loving energy. When my first cousins moved in with us as our family just started, I didn't hear any resentment in her voice or detect any anger or disappointment. All she did was embrace them with love and kindness. A mother is the heart of the family, and when the heart is good and strong, you can weather any circumstance. Her open heart, kindness, and love are expressed and felt by everyone in our family.

Uata/I Don't Remember My Father's Face

Lu'isa and her sisters. From right to left: Losaline, Lu'isa, Sepiuta & 'Olivia

Lu'isa shared this song that she often sang with her sisters. It was a song her father composed and dedicated to their late mom in memory of her. In it, he expresses her worth as a mother and that she is dearly missed on Mother's Day. The lyrics are as follows:

> 1. 'Ofa atu si'eku fa'e, 'ise'isa teke ngalo nai 'afe
> Love expressed to you, dear mother, and how can I forget
> Ho'o 'ofa mo ho'o ngaue, 'oku malohi ange ia he mate
> Your love and your work are stronger than death.
> 2. 'Isa kuo langalanga noa, si'ete manatu mo si'ete 'ofa
> Oh, the lingering feeling as I recall your memory and your love
> Ki si'i fa'e si'ono fofonga, faka'ofo'ofa ange ia he maka koloa
> To mother, your face is more beautiful than rocks of treasures.
> 3. Toki 'aho mamahi e, si'a taha kuo 'ikai si'ane fa'e
> What a mournful day for someone with no mother
> Toki mahu'inga he'ene mole, ka kuo hola ia 'o fiemalie
> Treasure has been recognized too late, but she has now gone off to rest in peace.
> Chorus: 'Uluaki 'Otua 'ae fa'e, kakato 'oe ikuna kotoa pe
> First God is mother, all achievements conquered

Unsung Hero

Fa'unga 'o natula ke laka hake, sino moe laumalie
Natural composite to build up, body, and spirit.

Uliti and Luisa on the first opening of Parliament in his first term

As the old saying goes, "Behind every great man is an incredible woman"; Lu'isa is that and so much more. Her demeanor is always loving, her understanding is remarkable, her heart as pure as snow. No matter how much or how often I messed up, Lu'isa encouraged me to stop dwelling on failures and get up and try again. Every night before we went to sleep, she would rub her hands over my head, give me a massage and say, "This is the smartest brain in the world, and it's all wrapped up in this beautiful head of yours, 'Uliti." When I downplayed her words, she would repeat herself until I acknowledged what she said. Failure is not in Lu'isa's vocabulary. To her, failure is an opportunity to do things all over again but better because now you have experience.

Lu'isa is the hardest-working woman I know. She's the first to rise in our household and the last to go to sleep. In the middle of the night, I would hear her tiptoe around, and when I asked what she was doing, she always answered, "I just needed to finish up a few things." It's like she sleeps, but her mind is on all the time, thinking about what our family needs.

I remember in the late 1970s, our business was struggling to stay afloat. Lu'isa was in the US at the time giving birth to our twin boys, Douglas and Arthur, and I wrote to her a letter explaining my frustration that we may be facing the brink of bankruptcy. I poured my heart and soul into this letter about the government being a fierce competitor and slapping me with fees left and right and on and on.

She called me and said, "'Uliti, I don't know about you, but I will speak with Joshua in the Bible, 'Choose you this day whom ye will serve…but as for me and my house, we will serve the Lord.'" (Joshua king james version, chapter24, verse15, 2001)[87] Lu'isa continued, "'Uliti, I can hear the fear in your voice and defeat in your words. No one can do this to you except yourself. Do not allow this circumstance to beat you down. We've been through much worse. I have said this before, but I will say it again when you have reached the end of your rope, and you have done everything that is humanly possible, this is when you enact your faith in action because when man ends, God begins."

Lu'isa's words were as fierce as rolling thunder and jolted my sense back as I realized it was Satan's tactics to have my mind feel defeated and keep me in a never-ending loop of negative thoughts. Lu'isa also reminded me that failure is part of life experiences, but if you fail and stay in that stage, then it's a failure, but if you fail, then get up again and say, it's all right, this was just an experience to learn from my mistake, then it's not a failure but a lesson learned.

Although I know what faith means, Lu'isa takes this concept to a whole new level, and with that, I had to reread what the Bible says about faith: "Now faith is the substance of things hoped for, the evidence of things not seen." (Hebrews king james version, chapter11 verse1 , 2001)[88] Rereading the definition of faith made me realize that Lu'isa does not rely on her five senses when it comes to faith. She relies on her intuition and what she deeply believes in. Although she has often not seen things manifest, she still believes it will happen, and that's how faith has played a vital role throughout her life.

Even when our marriage was rocky at times due to temptations and my shortcomings as a man, Lu'isa never held it against me. Even when I was in a fallen state and everyone else condemned me, Lu'isa did not. She has always forgiven me fully and many times over as she said, "'Uliti, there is no perfect person alive." The only perfect person was Jesus Christ. All of us, including you and I, must realize that this is the reason why our Savior came and died for our sins, so we may be redeemed in the eyes of our Heavenly Father. The Bible tells us that our Savior did not come for the righteous but for the sinner to repent.

One of Lu'isa's favorite parables in the Bible is the story told in John 8 where the scribes and Pharisees brought an adulterous woman to be stoned to death according to Moses' laws. Jesus was writing on the ground, and as he rose, "…he lifted up himself, and said unto them, He that is without sin among you, let him first cast a stone at her." (John king james version, chapter8, verse7 , 2001)[89] Jesus stooped down and again wrote on the ground while each one left one by one, and at the end, none of the accusers remained.

No matter what issues we face, whether it's big or small, we manage to overcome them because of Lu'isa's forgiving heart. She would often say, who am I to judge as who will judge me? Her positive attitude is infectious, and it allows us to stay the course and smooth out any issues that may stand to destroy our marriage. Lu'isa often says that love conquers all, and whatever life throws at our family, she says her love is stronger than the adversary. She often quotes from the scriptures 1 Corinthians 13:1-13

> 1 Though I speak with the tongues of men and of angels and have not charity, I have become as sounding brass or a tinkling cymbal.
>
> 2 And though I have the gift of prophecy and understand all mysteries and knowledge; and though I have all faith so that I could remove mountains and have not charity, I am nothing.
>
> 3 And though I bestow all my goods to feed the poor, and though I give my body to be burned, and have not charity, it profiteth me nothing.
>
> 4 Charity suffereth long, and is kind; charity envieth not; charity vaunteth, not itself, is not puffed up,
>
> 5 Doth not behave itself unseemly, seeketh not her own, is not easily provoked, thinketh no evil;
>
> 6 Rejoiceth not in iniquity, but rejoiceth in the truth;
>
> 7 Beareth all things, believeth all things, hopeth all things, endureth all things.
>
> 8 Charity never faileth: but whether there be prophecies, they shall fail; whether there be tongues,

they shall cease; whether there be knowledge, it shall vanish away.

11 When I was a child, I spoke as a child, I understood as a child, I thought as a child: but when I became a man, I put away childish things.

13 And now abideth faith, hope, charity, these three; but the greatest of these is charity. (1 Corinthians king james version, chapter13, verses1-13, 2001)[90]

Lu'isa has many talents; among them are dancing, music, and poetry. She can hit high notes and harmonize with others through acapella. She can recite a poem at a drop of a hat, and she makes it sound so effortless. When our children were young, once a week, we had a family home evening on Mondays, and each child had to stand up and do a number, whether it was dancing or singing a song, but everyone had to perform. This was her way of encouraging the children to discover their God-given talents. She's a fierce competitor, and she does her best in anything and everything that she does as she always brings her A-game to the task at hand. She loves to play cards and once she's got you hooked into a game of cards, prepare to stay for hours or until she wins.

Lu'isa has a special place in her heart for widows. Every Mother's Day and Christmas, she starts to prepare for her baking the day before, then she wakes up before dawn the morning of and begins baking for all the widows in our ward. After she is done, she loads the baked goods into her van and hauls it to drop off a basket of baked goods to each widow. Even to this day, she still does these types of services on her own, as in Lu'isa's own words, "It brings me great joy when I hand off the baked goods to the widows." She said, "It's not so much for the baked goods, but to tell the widows they're not forgotten and that someone loves and cares for them." Lu'isa talks the talk and walks the walk.

There isn't anything Lu'isa teaches our children unless she does it first. Then she says, "Now you've seen me do it. Follow my example." This is a powerful way of teaching concepts and principles to our children where they learn by seeing what their mother has done. If any one of our children goes to complain about one of their siblings to Lu'isa, she hears them out, then she will point out the strength of that particular child they're complaining about. In her loving way, Lu'isa accepts everyone for who they are without judgment. She only sees the goodness in people, and she's quick to point out their strengths. She is a natural cheerleader as she can turn a frown upside down and make you smile as she talks about your strength until you walk away feeling all high and mighty.

Lu'isa and I have been married for sixty-plus years, have eleven children, six boys and five girls, and here are their names from oldest to youngest in order of their birth:

Venisi Jr	February 9th, 1961
Mele Lavinia	September 4th, 1962
Melenaite Sr	June 26th, 1964
Tevita Tu'i	September 26th, 1964
Thomas S Monson	August 27th, 1968
Edward Kay	February 9th, 1970
Melelupe	April 2nd, 1975
Douglas 'Ofa-ki-Ha'angana	January 30th, 1977
Arthur Paea-'i-Vahamama'o	January 30th, 1977
Melenaite Jr	February 27th, 1983
Lucynita Murley	June 9th, 1988

Uata Family Photo taken in our 2019 Family Reunion in Tonga

We have sixty-plus grandchildren and thirty-four-plus great-grandchildren and counting. Even through the turbulent waters of life, we managed to stay together as a family because Lu'isa is the glue that held us together. I am forever grateful to have Lu'isa by my side, who stood by me regardless of all of my flaws. She is a woman of God, a woman of strength, and a woman of faith. With all the sincerity of my heart, I thank her for being the queen of our family. If I were to describe Lu'isa, the words of Proverbs speak volumes to her character:

> [10] Who can find a virtuous woman? For her price is far above rubies.
>
> [11] The heart of her husband doth safely trust in her so that he shall have no need of spoil.
>
> [12] She will do him good and not evil all the days of her life.
>
> [17] She girdeth her loins with strength and strengtheneth her arms.
>
> [20] She stretcheth out her hand to the poor; yea, she reacheth forth her hands to the needy.
>
> [25] Strength and honour are her clothing, and she shall rejoice in time to come.
>
> [26] She openeth her mouth with wisdom, and in her tongue is the law of kindness.
>
> [27] She looketh well to the ways of her household, and eateth not the bread of idleness.
>
> [28] Her children arise up and call her blessed; her husband also, and he praiseth her.
>
> [30] Favour is deceitful, and beauty is vain: but a woman that feareth the Lord, she shall be praised. (Proverbs king james version, chapter31, 2001)[91]

Lu'isa is the unsung hero in our family. She is the epitome of a daughter, mother, grandmother, great-grandmother, and wife as she embodies all the Christ-like characteristics aforementioned. She is the embodiment of charity as she has always put everyone else's needs before her own. Even if it meant her pride, happiness, or well-being, she has sacrificed and dedicated her whole life to make sure the Uata Family stays together as we have been sealed in the temple of God for time and all eternity, and families are forever. The End

Uata Children: starting from back row right to left: 'Etu, Soni, Tu'i, Naite Lahi, Lavi, Venisi. 2nd row left to right: Lucy, Lu'isa (mom), 'Uliti (dad), Naite Si'i. front row: 'Afa & Melelupe

Family Photo Album

granddaughters, Alex on right, Pua in middle and Mona on left performed a Tongan tau'olunga on 'Uliti's 80th birthday celebration

Walter Harold Murley is 'Uliti's grandfather and he was an adventurous man. He sailed from England to all over the Pacific in the early 1900's and stopped by Tonga

Walter married a Tongan lady named Manu Vahetoa and had Lisiate then he continued his explorer while Lisiate remained in Tonga with his mother then he later married Melepua and had Venisi and 'Uliti

Family Photo Album

2006 Uata Reunion held at Ha'ano, Ha'apai—picture at family graveyard

'Uliti Uata

Picture of Nuku'alofa comparison on same spot in 1950 and in 2020

1995 Uata Reunion

Lu'isa and 'Uliti in the 70's

Naite Lahi in the middle and Taki and 'Afa when they were little

'Uliti's 83rd birthday celebration—grandkids sitting on floor with pink outfits

Lu'isa's 80th birthday celebration

Family picture at reunion in Tonga1

Family picture at reunion in Tonga2

Family picture at reunion in Tonga3

Melelupe at 'Uliti's 83rd birthday

In-laws of the Uata Family

Family Photo Album

Tu'i and Peta

'Uliti, Lu'isa and Mona in front of our home in Tonga--Dec 25th, 2021

'Uliti, Lu'isa and Lome at our home in Tonga—Dec 25th, 2021

Sunrise picture at our home in Tonga— Oct 2021

Uata grandchildren —2021 celebrating Richie's birthday in Tonga

Uata grandchildren-- 2021 celebrating Lillian's 21st birthday in Las Vegas

Images of Tonga

Tonga Coat of Arms
Image courtesy:
https://upload.wikimedia.org/wikipedia/commons/thumb/4/43/Coat_of_arms_of_Tonga.svg/433px-Coat_of_arms_of_Tonga.svg.png

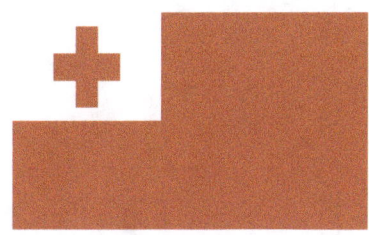

Flag of Tonga
Image courtesy:
https://upload.wikimedia.org/wikipedia/commons/9/9a/Flag_of_Tonga.svg

Tonga Palace
Image courtesy:
https://upload.wikimedia.org/wikipedia/commons/thumb/9/94/Royal_Palace%2C_Nuku%27alofa%2C_Nov_18.jpg/330px-Royal_Palace%2C_Nuku%27alofa%2C_Nov_18.jpg

Princess Salote Mafile'o Pilolevu married to Hon. Siosaia Ma'ulupekotofa Tuita in 1976
Image courtesy:
https://en.wikipedia.org/wiki/Salote_Mafile%CA%BBo_Pilolevu_Tuita#/media/File:Royal_Tongan_Wedding_of_1976.jpg

Girls doing the Tongan tau'olunga
Image courtesy:
https://en.wikipedia.org/wiki/Tonga#/media/File:Ula_fu.jpg

Nuku Island in Vava'u, Tonga
Image courtesy:
https://upload.wikimedia.org/wikipedia/commons/3/3d/Nuku_Island_Vava%27u.jpg

References

1 Corinthians king james version, chapter13, verses1-13. (2001, january 1). Retrieved from king james bible online: https://www.kingjamesbibleonline.org/1-Corinthians-Chapter-13/

1 Timothy king james version, chapter6, verses 6-9. (2001, january 31). Retrieved from king james bible online: https://www.kingjamesbibleonline.org/1-Timothy-Chapter-6/#6

2 Corinthians king james version. (2001, january 31). Retrieved from king james bible online: https://www.kingjamesbibleonline.org/2-Corinthians-Chapter-9/#7

2022, A. P. (2009, august 20). *Ferry too deep for divers*. Retrieved from otago daily times: https://www.odt.co.nz/news/national/ferry-too-deep-divers

A prayer of St. Francis of Assisi. (2021, january 6). Retrieved from wikisource: https://en.wikisource.org/wiki/A_prayer_of_St._Francis_of_Assisi

Akilisi acquitted on defamation charges. (1998, april 27). Retrieved from matangitonga: https://matangitonga.to/1998/04/27/akilisi-acquitted-defamation-charges

Albert Einstein. (2021, September 30). Retrieved from wikiquote: https://en.wikiquote.org/w/index.php?title=Albert_Einstein&oldid=3010679

albert einstein. (2022, february 1). Retrieved from wikiquote: https://en.wikiquote.org/wiki/Albert_Einstein#Quotes

Book of Mormon chapter18. (2000, january 1). Retrieved from the church of jesus christ of later-day saints: https://www.churchofjesuschrist.org/study/scriptures/bofm/mosiah/18?lang=eng

Book of Mormon, chapter 12. (2019, july 1). Retrieved from the church of jesus christ of later day saints: https://www.churchofjesuschrist.org/study/scriptures/bofm/ether/12?lang=eng

References

Book of Mormon, chapter2. (2001, january 31). Retrieved from the church of jesus christ of later days saints: https://www.churchofjesuschrist.org/study/scriptures/bofm/2-ne/2.25?lang=eng#p24

Contentment. (2021, August 22). Retrieved from wikiquote: https://en.wikiquote.org/w/index.php?title=Contentment&oldid=2997720

count your blessings. (2022, february 2). Retrieved from song select by CCLI: https://songselect.ccli.com/Songs/40416/count-your-blessings

doctrine and covenants 59. (2019, june 26). Retrieved from the church of jesus christ of later day saints: https://www.churchofjesuschrist.org/study/scriptures/dc-testament/dc/59?lang=eng

Ecclesiastes king james version chapter3 verse1. (2001, january 31). Retrieved from king james bible online: https://www.kingjamesbibleonline.org/Ecclesiastes-3-1/

Ecclesiastes king james version, chapter3, verse1. (2009, november 1). Retrieved from king james bible online: https://www.kingjamesbibleonline.org/Ecclesiastes-3-1/

einstein, a. (2022, february 12). *albert einstein quotes*. Retrieved from godreads: https://www.goodreads.com/author/quotes/9810.Albert_Einstein

evangelist st., m. t. (2001, january 31). *matthew king james version chapter 26 verse 39*. Retrieved from king james bible online: https://www.kingjamesbibleonline.org/Matthew-Chapter-26/#39

Evangelist, J. t. (2001, january 31). *john king james version chapter3 verse 16*. Retrieved from king james bible online: https://www.kingjamesbibleonline.org/1-John-Chapter-3/

Evangelist, L. t. (2001, january 31). *luke king james version*. Retrieved from king james bible online: https://www.kingjamesbibleonline.org/Luke-15-4/

evangelist, l. t. (2001, january 31). *luke king james version chapter 10*. Retrieved from king james bible online: https://www.kingjamesbibleonline.org/Luke-Chapter-10/

evangelist, l. t. (2001, january 31). *luke king james version chapter 10*. Retrieved from king james bible online: https://www.kingjamesbibleonline.org/Luke-Chapter-10/

evangelist, l. t. (2001, january 31). *luke king james version chapter 23 verse 46*. Retrieved from king james bible online: https://www.kingjamesbibleonline.org/Luke-Chapter-23/#46

Evangelist, L. t. (2001, january 31). *Luke king james version, chapter17, verse15*. Retrieved from king james bible online: https://www.kingjamesbibleonline.org/Luke-17-15/

evangelist, s. m. (2001, january 31). *Matthew king james version chapter25 verse30*. Retrieved from king james bible online: https://www.kingjamesbibleonline.org/Matthew-Chapter-25/#30

evangelist, s. m. (2001, january 31). *Matthew king james version, chapter 17, verse20*. Retrieved from king james bible online: https://www.kingjamesbibleonline.org/Matthew-17-20/

evangelist, s. m. (2001, january 31). *matthew king james version, chapter6, verses19-21*. Retrieved from king james bible online: https://www.kingjamesbibleonline.org/Matthew-Chapter-6/

evangelist, s. m. (2009, september 6). *Matthew king james version, chapter11, verse5*. Retrieved from king james bible online : https://www.kingjamesbibleonline.org/Matthew-11-5/

File:Salote Tupou III of Tonga in coronation robe-crop. (2020, November 30). Retrieved from wikimedia commons: https://commons.wikimedia.org/wiki/File:Salote_Tupou_III_of_Tonga_in_coronation_robe-crop.jpg

Galatians king james version, chapter5, verse7. (2001, january 31). Retrieved from king james bible online: https://www.kingjamesbibleonline.org/Galatians-5-7/

Galatians king james version, chapter6, verse7. (2001, january 31). Retrieved from king james bible online: https://www.kingjamesbibleonline.org/Galatians-6-7/

Galatians king james version, chapter6, verse7. (2001, january 31). Retrieved from king james bible online: https://www.kingjamesbibleonline.org/Galatians-6-7/

Hebrews king james version, chapter11 verse1 . (2001, january 31). Retrieved from king james bible online: https://www.kingjamesbibleonline.org/Hebrews-11-1/

References

Henry VIII (play). (2021, October 10). Retrieved from wikiquote: https://en.wikipedia.org/w/index.php?title=Henry_VIII_(play)&oldid=1049278288

Isaac Newton. (2021, August 2). Retrieved from wikiquote: https://en.wikiquote.org/w/index.php?title=Isaac_Newton&oldid=2990419

It's Up to You. (n.d.). Retrieved from alaura1942.tripod: https://alaura1942.tripod.com/ItsUpToYou.html

Jeremiah king james version, chapter1, verse5. (2001, january 31). Retrieved from king james bible online: https://www.kingjamesbibleonline.org/Jeremiah-1-5/

JOB kings james version chapter2 verse10. (2001, january 31). Retrieved from king james bible online: https://www.kingjamesbibleonline.org/Job-2-10/

John king james version, chapter8, verse7. (2001, january 31). Retrieved from king james bible online: https://www.kingjamesbibleonline.org/John-8-7/

John of Salisbury. (2021, August 5). Retrieved from wikiquote: https://en.wikiquote.org/w/index.php?title=John_of_Salisbury&oldid=2992206

Joshua king james version, chapter24, verse15. (2001, january 31). Retrieved from king james bible online: https://www.kingjamesbibleonline.org/Joshua-24-15/

Jr., o. R. (2016, January 30). *The Oak Tree*. Retrieved from wiki freephile.org: https://wiki.freephile.org/wiki/The_Oak_Tree

Jury clears Pohivas in sedition trial. (2003, august 30). Retrieved from matangitonga: https://matangitonga.to/2003/08/30/jury-clears-pohivas-sedition-trial

Ko e fasi 'o e tu'i 'o e 'Otu Tonga. (2022, January 29). Retrieved from wikipedia: https://en.wikipedia.org/wiki/Ko_e_fasi_%CA%BBo_e_tu%CA%BBi_%CA%BBo_e_%CA%BBOtu_Tonga

KO E TOHI HIMI (SIASI UESILIANA TAU'ATAINA 'O TONGA. (n.d.). Retrieved from academia.edu: https://www.academia.edu/38989670/KO_E_TOHI_HIMI_SIASI_UESILIANA_TAUATAINA_O_TONGA

Liuaki, T. (n.d.). Taufa'ahau, Tu'i Ha'apai.

matthew, t. e. (1611). chapter 10, verse 25. In t. e. matthew, *matthew king james version*.

matthew, t. e. (2001, january 31). *matthew king james version chapter 17, verse 20*. Retrieved from king james bible online: https://www.kingjamesbibleonline.org/Matthew-Chapter-17/#20

matthew, t. E. (2001, january 31). *matthew king james version chapter 8*. Retrieved from king james bible online: file:///C:/Users/nidhi/Desktop/mendeley/reference%201 html

matthew, t. e. (2001, january 31). *matthew king james version chapter25 verse40*. Retrieved from king james bible online: https://www.kingjamesbibleonline.org/Matthew-25-40/

Mifflin, H. (n.d.). *Irish Proverbs & Sayings*. Retrieved from irish culture and customs: https://www.irishcultureandcustoms.com/Quotes/ProvbsSayings html

moses. (2001, january 31). *genesis king james version chapter48 verse17*. Retrieved from king james bible online: https://www.kingjamesbibleonline.org/Genesis-Chapter-48/#17

Mothers. (2021, October 11). Retrieved from wikiquote: https://en.wikiquote.org/w/index.php?title=Mothers&oldid=3017002

Philippians king james version, chapter4, verses 11-13. (2009, august 7). Retrieved from king james bible: https://www.kingjamesbibleonline.org/Philippians-Chapter-4/

Proverbs king james version, chapter 15. (2001, january 31). Retrieved from king james bible online: https://www.kingjamesbibleonline.org/Proverbs-Chapter-15/#4

Proverbs king james version, chapter23, verse7. (2001, january 31). Retrieved from king james bible online: https://www.kingjamesbibleonline.org/Proverbs-23-7/

Proverbs king james version, chapter31. (2001, january 31). Retrieved from king james bible online: https://www.kingjamesbibleonline.org/Proverbs-Chapter-31/

Psalms king james version, chapter37, verse 4. (2001, january 31). Retrieved from king james bible online: https://www.kingjamesbibleonline.org/Psalms-37-4/

References

Ray, J. (31 August 2008, August 31). Photograph of MV Princess Ashika pier side at Natovi Landing. *Wikipedia*.

(2010). *Royal Commission of Inquiry into the Sinking of the MV Princess Ashika.* nuku'alofa, kingdom of tonga. Retrieved from ndhadeliver.natlib.govt nz: https://ndhadeliver natlib.govt nz/delivery/DeliveryManagerServlet?dps_pid=IE1601671

(2010). *Royal Commission of Inquiry into the Sinking of the MV Princess Ashika.* nuku'alofa, kingdom of tonga.

(2010). *Royal Commission of Inquiry into the Sinking of the MV Princess Ashika.* nuku'alofa, kingdom of tonga.

Russell Conwel. (2019, December 14). Retrieved from wikiquote: https://en.wikiquote.org/w/index.php?title=Russell_Conwell&oldid=2710664

Samuel. (2001, january 31). *samuel king james version chapter16 verse7*. Retrieved from king james bible online: https://www.kingjamesbibleonline.org/1-Samuel-Chapter-16/#7

serenity prayer. (2021, october 28). Retrieved from wikipedia: https://en.wikipedia.org/wiki/Serenity_Prayer

solomon. (2001, january 31). *proverbs, king james version*. Retrieved from king james bible: https://www.kingjamesbibleonline.org/Proverbs-Chapter-15/#4

Søren Kierkegaard. (2021, https://en.wikiquote.org/w/index.php?title=S%C3%B8ren_Kierkegaard&oldid=3001484 2). Retrieved from wikiquote: https://en.wikiquote.org/w/index.php?title=S%C3%B8ren_Kierkegaard&oldid=3001484

Spink, K. (n.d.). *Mother Teresa: An Authorized Biography*. newyork: HarperOne.

That's What Faith Must Be. (2017, january 14). Retrieved from genius: https://genius.com/Michael-card-thats-what-faith-must-be-lyrics

Tongan protest marchers call for political reform. (2006, june 1). Retrieved from matangitonga: https://matangitonga.to/2006/06/01/tongan-protest-marchers-call-political-reform

Tonga's civil servants decide to continue strike. (2005, august 10). Retrieved from matangitonga: https://matangitonga.to/comment/795#comment-795

Tuku fonua : the land given to God. (2019, january 7). Retrieved from worldcat: https://www.worldcat.org/title/tuku-fonua-the-land-given-to-god/oclc/152666931

Tuku fonua : the land given to God. (2019, january 7). Retrieved from worldcat: https://www.worldcat.org/title/tuku-fonua-the-land-given-to-god/oclc/152666931

Washington Irving. (2021, march 18). Retrieved from wikiquote: https://en.wikiquote.org/w/index.php?title=Washington_Irving&oldid=2940628

Wikipedia, t. f. (2020, december 6). *MV Princess Ashika.* Retrieved from Wikipedia: https://en.wikipedia.org/w/index.php?title=MV_Princess_Ashika&oldid=992605466

wikipedia, t. f. (2020, November 26). *Tevita Tu'i Uata.* Retrieved from wikipedia: https://en.wikipedia.org/wiki/Tevita_Tu%27i_Uata

Wikipedia, t. f. (2021, September 9). *Albert Pike.* Retrieved from Wikipedia: https://en.wikipedia.org/w/index.php?title=Albert_Pike&oldid=1043317490

Wikipedia, t. f. (2021, September 22). *I Have a Dream.* Retrieved from Wikipedia: https://en.wikipedia.org/w/index.php?title=I_Have_a_Dream&oldid=1045787362

Wikipedia, t. f. (2021, september 30). *Mahatma Gandhi.* Retrieved from Wikipedia: https://en.wikipedia.org/w/index.php?title=Mahatma_Gandhi&oldid=1047387811

Wikipedia, t. f. (2021, september 28). *Martin Luther King Jr.* Retrieved from Wikipedia: https://en.wikipedia.org/w/index.php?title=Martin_Luther_King_Jr.&oldid=1047008435

Wikipedia, t. f. (2021, August 29). *Missionaries of Charity.* Retrieved from Wikipedia:

References

https://en.wikipedia.org/w/index.php?title=Missionaries_of_Charity&oldid=1041335022

Wikipedia, t. f. (2021, september 24). *Mother Teresa*. Retrieved from Wikipedia: https://en.wikipedia.org/w/index.php?title=Mother_Teresa&oldid=1046112957

Wikipedia, t. f. (2021, September 13). *Nelson Mandela*. Retrieved from wikipedia: https://en.wikipedia.org/w/index.php?title=Nelson_Mandela&oldid=1044097208

Wikipedia, t. f. (2021, October 9). *Serenity Prayer*. Retrieved from Wikipedia: https://en.wikipedia.org/w/index.php?title=Serenity_Prayer&oldid=1048996309

Wikipedia, t. f. (2021, December 16). *The Star Thrower*. Retrieved from Wikipedia: https://en.wikipedia.org/wiki/The_Star_Thrower#The_story_as_adapted

wikipedia, t. f. (2021, may 7). *Tongan Kava Ceremony-Taumafa Kava*. Retrieved from wikipedia: https://en.wikipedia.org/wiki/Tongan_Kava_Ceremony-Taumafa_Kava

wikipedia, t. f. (2021, may 7). *Tongan Kava Ceremony-Taumafa Kava*. Retrieved from wikipedia: https://en.wikipedia.org/wiki/Tongan_Kava_Ceremony-Taumafa_Kava#/media/File:George_Tupou_I,_c._1880s.jpg

Wikipedia, t. f. (2022, January 19). *2006 Nukuʻalofa riots*. Retrieved from wikipedia: https://en.wikipedia.org/wiki/2006_Nuku%CA%BBalofa_riots

Wikipedia, t. f. (2022, January 30). *Akilisi Pōhiva*. Retrieved from wikipedia: https://en.wikipedia.org/wiki/%CA%BBAkilisi_P%C5%8Dhiva

Wikipedia, t. f. (2022, January 30). *Akilisi Pōhiva*. Retrieved from Wikipedia: https://en.wikipedia.org/wiki/%CA%BBAkilisi_P%C5%8Dhiva

Wikipedia, t. f. (2022, February 1). *history of tonga*. Retrieved from wikipedia: https://en.wikipedia.org/wiki/History_of_Tonga

wikipedia, t. f. (2022, january 19). *Lakalaka*. Retrieved from wikipedia: https://en.wikipedia.org/wiki/Lakalaka#Choreography

Wikipedia, t. f. (2022, January 17). *Maya Angelou*. Retrieved from Wikipedia: https://en.wikipedia.org/w/index.php?title=Maya_Angelou&oldid=1066158699

Wikipedia, t. f. (2022, January 5). *Uliti Uata*. Retrieved from Wikipedia: https://en.wikipedia.org/wiki/%CA%BBUliti_Uata